REINVENTION

Stories from an Urban Church

Mark is a leader, an entrepreneur, and a scientist with a pastor's heart. He leads us on a journey where the future creates the present – the eschatological hope and vision that shatters the doubt and negativity of the past. Mark does not know the meaning of "it's not possible."
– Rev. Gregor Sneddon, Rector at St. Luke's Ottawa

How refreshing to read a story that runs against the familiar tropes of inevitable church decay and decline! Mark Whittall's account of planting a new church in a tough context is the story of creative pastoral sagacity – an ability to reimagine church and to bring a vision to birth. It is the story of a distinctively Anglican church plant – rooted in place, nourished by the great traditions of liturgy and sacrament, unafraid of the best insights of the human sciences, and committed to justice for all; yet also one that relates those orientations to the realities of the congregation's contemporary urban milieu. We can be grateful that the insights that have arisen from this adventure are made available to a wider public in an engaging, accessible prose.
– Kevin Flynn, Director, Anglican Studies Program, Saint Paul University, Ottawa

Mark Whittall

ReInvention

Stories from an Urban Church

WOOD LAKE

Editor: Mike Schwartzentruber
Designer: Robert MacDonald
Proofreader: Dianne Greenslade

Library and Archives Canada Cataloguing in Publication
Whittall, Mark, 1962-, author
ReInvention : stories from an urban church / Mark Whittall.
Includes bibliographical references.
Issued in print and electronic formats.
ISBN 978-1-77064-805-0 (paperback). – ISBN 978-1-77064-806-7 (html)
1. Church of St. Alban the Martyr (Ottawa, Ont.). 2. Church development,
New – Ontario – Ottawa. 3. Church renewal – Anglican Church of Canada.
4. Church renewal – Ontario – Ottawa. 5. Church work – Anglican Communion.
6. Christian leadership. 7. City churches – Ontario – Ottawa. I. Title.
BX5617.O8S17 2016   283'.71384   C2015-908074-6   C2015-908075-4

Unless otherwise noted, scripture quotations are from the *New Revised
Standard Version* of the Bible, copyright 1983, Division of Christian
Education of the National Council of Churches of Christ in the United
States of America. All rights reserved. Used by permission. Permission has
also been gratefully received from the following people for the use of their
material in this book: Paula Best, Ins Choi, Kelly Egan, Barbara Brown
Taylor, Jonathan Harris of 9th Hour Theatre, and Hallie Cotnam.

ISBN 978-1-77064-805-0

Published by Wood Lake Publishing Inc.
485 Beaver Lake Road, Kelowna, BC, Canada, V4V 1S5
www.woodlake.com | 250.766.2778

We acknowledge the financial support of the Government of Canada. Nous
reconnaissons l'appui financier du gouvernement du Canada. Wood Lake
Publishing acknowledges the financial support of the Province of British
Columbia through the Book Publishing Tax Credit.

At Wood Lake Publishing, we practice what we publish, being guided by a
concern for fairness, justice, and equal opportunity in all of our
relationships with employees and customers. Wood Lake Publishing is
committed to caring for the environment and all creation. Wood Lake
Publishing recycles and reuses, and encourages readers to do the same.
Books are printed on 100% post-consumer recycled paper, whenever
possible. A percentage of all profit is donated to charitable organizations.

Printed in Canada. Printing 10 9 8 7 6 5 4 3 2

TABLE OF CONTENTS

DEDICATION

To Guylaine, Jonathan, and
Michelle, with thanks and love.

ACKNOWLEDGMENTS

The greatest weakness in writing an account of the beginnings of a new church community as a first person narrative is that it tends to overstate my role and perspective and to understate the invaluable leadership and contributions of a great many other people. *ReInvention* is my story, based on my experiences and my memories, and experience and memory are tricky things. There is an essential subjectivity about them, and so the stories I tell might be quite different from the way others would remember and speak of the same events. Their versions may well be closer to the truth.

The new beginning of St. Albans Church, which forms much of the subject matter of these stories, was from the start a team effort, both in its leadership and in its execution. In the spring of 2011, a core group of ten people came together to plan, launch, and build a new community: Andrew Stephens-Rennie, Ericka Stephens-Rennie, Rochelle Garner, Michael Garner, Ron Chaplin, Haig McCarrell, Romizah Walters, Matt Simmermon-Gomes, and Peter Cazaly. I was privileged to be a part of this amazing group. Each person brought his or her own incredible gifts and energy to the building of our community. Each brought their own vision of what church could be and *together* we were more than the sum of our parts. I owe these people a great deal. In addition to the role they played in building the St. Albans community, they also shaped me into a better person and a better church leader. Thank you. And thanks also to the many others, too many to name, who have joined us along the way. There are few things I value more than being part of the St. Albans community.

Many friends and colleagues contributed to the writing of this book. Thanks go to Ron Chaplin, Gregor Sneddon, Shaun Baron, Mary-Martha Hale, John Wright, Michael Garner, Rochelle Garner, Zack Ingles, Haig McCarrell, Sid Ypma, and Richard Bass, all of whom took the time to read the manuscript and provide valuable comments. Thanks also to Scott Evans for helpful advice and to Anne Louise Mahoney and Diana Butler Bass, whose encouragement kept this project going and led me to seek a publisher for the book. I am indebted to my bishop, John Chapman, who not only put me in position to write these stories, but who also read the manuscript and provided feedback, support, and encouragement along the way. Thanks also to Paula Best, Ins Choi, Kelly Egan, Barbara Brown Taylor, Jonathan Harris of 9th Hour Theatre, and Hallie Cotnam for permission to use their work in the text.

I appreciate all those who have listened to these stories in one form or another – in conversation, as homilies, as workshops or retreat presentations – especially the parish council of St. Luke's Ottawa, the people of St. Andrew's Presbyterian (Ottawa), colleagues from the Diocese of Montreal, and of course my own St. Albans community. Feedback from these encounters has shaped these pages. But more importantly, these conversations suggested to me that the stories from our urban church plant might well be useful and even inspiring to many who are wrestling with the need to change the way they do church in response to the new cultural climate in which we find ourselves. I know that many of my colleagues in ministry find themselves in situations more challenging than those I have faced. It is in many ways easier to plant a new church than to renew an existing congregation. My hope is that these stories may be a tool that church leaders who find themselves in a wide variety of situations can use to open up needed and life-giving conversations in their own congregations.

I'd like to express my appreciation and thanks to my editor Mike Schwartzentruber and to the team at Wood Lake Publishing. Mike has used his skills, patience, and attention to detail to turn my initial manuscript into this book, much-improved along the way. But more importantly, I always got the sense that he shared my passion for the things about which I have written, and his help and encouragement along the way have been invaluable. It has been a pleasure working with Mike, Kailee, Robert, Patty, Lynette, Deb and all the folks at Wood Lake Publishing.

Most importantly, I would like to thank my family for their love and support. My parents, Carole and Phil, have always been there for me, and that includes Sundays at St. Albans. My children, Jonathan and Michelle, are everything a father could hope for. They supported my transition into ordained ministry and provided great feedback on the manuscript. Michelle has been my in-house editor, providing wise comments page by page. And I am deeply indebted to my wife Guylaine, who has enabled me to complete this project by taking on so many other things. I couldn't have better companions on my journey. Thanks and love.

PREFACE

**The Church that we live and pray in today will
not look or feel the same in ten years.** That is to say, if we pray with
unceasing clarity, listen intently to the murmurings of a lively and
chaotic Spirit of God, attune ourselves to the public square, and be
mindful of the needs of religious people and those seeking God in
these times, our church communities will be more vibrant and more
faithful but very different. And if we do not do these things, the
Church will become a historic relic that merely reminds us of what
we used to do in early days and leave us wondering why it is not
working today.

The Rev. Mark Whittall, in this monograph, *Reinvention: Stories
from an Urban Church*, calls us to all this and more in an engaging
and attractive manner. Mark, a priest in the Diocese of Ottawa of
which I am currently the bishop, assumed leadership and responsibility of an empty building, St. Albans, located in Ottawa's downtown
core. He was charged with the task of building (planting) a vibrant
mission-focused community of holy people that long to be faithful to
the mission of God in today's multicultural, multi-religious and diverse society. He challenges the faithful, challenges the church institution and challenges the growing number of seekers and members
of this "new creation" to be bold, to take risks but to be always mindful of God's call to love God and love our neighbour, and be faithful
stewards of the gifts God has given to all of us.

Mark's good nature, wit and wisdom draw us forward, page after page to journey with him and the community of St. Albans. We

must journey with them because the challenges he and the people of St. Albans face are the same challenges faithful Christians across the land face in their parishes and in those parishes we imagine might exist some day. This is a hopeful story, a Godly story, and a human story. It is a worthwhile read for all who seek God in community and those who struggle to know God more fully.

The Rt. Rev. Dr. John H. Chapman
9th Bishop of the Diocese of Ottawa
November 17, 2015

PROLOGUE

"Don't Let It Get Weird"

I stood up to go. As I did, Bishop John gave me one last piece of advice: "Just don't let it get weird." With those words ringing in my ears, I took my leave and headed out on my church planting adventure.

It's not like I hadn't seen it coming. The day before there had been an urgent phone call from the bishop's office.

"The bishop would like to see you early next week."

"Next week I'll be in Nicaragua. I'm taking my youth group there on a school-building trip. If it's urgent I can come in tomorrow."

"Come in tomorrow."

I turned to my wife, Guylaine: "Looks like I'm getting a new job – it's either St. Thomas or St. Albans and I'm pretty sure it's not St. Thomas."

The phone call was a surprise, but I'd known that *something* was about to happen. As a member of our diocesan council, I'd been briefed regularly about the St. Albans negotiations. I was also part of the communications team that had been hastily thrown together when the plan to move our day program for those experiencing homelessness back to St. Albans had suddenly become front-page news.

The Church of St. Alban the Martyr was, after Christ Church Cathedral, the second Anglican parish to be established in Ottawa in 1865. Construction of the church building began in 1867 to accommodate the influx of labourers, public servants, and soldiers, who flooded the city when Queen Victoria, in an unexpected move, named Ottawa the new capital of the fledgling Dominion of Canada. Before long, a number of prominent citizens, including Canada's first prime minister, Sir John A. Macdonald, made St. Albans their church home.

At the insistence of its first rector, the Reverend Thomas Bedford-Jones, St. Albans was a "rent-free" church. The custom in those days was to have pews rented and reserved by the wealthy, with the pews at the front commanding the highest prices. In the new church of St. Alban the Martyr, there would be no rental of pews. People would be able to sit wherever they wanted, rich and poor together. This was a radical innovation in the 19th century, a gospel stand that deprived the parish of an important revenue stream and left it perpetually strapped for cash in its early days.

In 2007, in another seemingly radical innovation, the Anglican Diocese of Ottawa took its first tentative step towards the blessing of same-sex civil marriages at its 126th annual synod meeting. This was intended as a pastoral response to the needs of LGBTQ (Lesbian, Gay, Bisexual, Transgender, or Queer) folk, an effort to be welcoming, affirming and inclusive. In response, the congregation and priest of St. Alban the Martyr voted to leave the Diocese of Ottawa and the Anglican Church of Canada at their 2008 annual meeting. As one might expect, there were hard feelings and disagreements over finances and property. To the credit of people on both sides of the dispute, the disagreements were kept out of the courts, and eventually a team of people from the congregation and the diocese sat down to negotiate a resolution. By early 2011, the resolution, and the return of the church building to the diocese, were within sight. We were getting our building back. But what were we going to do with it?

Around the same time that the St. Albans negotiations were

churning their way towards an eventual agreement, Centre 454 was on the look-out for a new home. The Centre's lease was about to expire and it had outgrown its space on Murray Street, in the Ottawa neighbourhood of Lowertown.

Centre 454 started in 1954 as a ministry of the Anglican Church in Ottawa to help men leaving the prison system integrate back into society. Over the past 60 years, it has grown and evolved into a day program that provides drop-in support, social recreation, and a wide range of services to assist individuals who are experiencing homelessness or living in poverty. As in many North American cities, homelessness is a major problem in Ottawa, and the Centre serves up to 200 people each day. Over the course of a year, approximately 7,000 people find themselves homeless in the city. Centre 454 provides these and other vulnerable people with a place to go during the day, somewhere they can check email or use a phone; take a shower; access counselling, mental health, and medical services; get assistance with housing or employment; or simply have a coffee and play some cards. Many of the participants consider the Centre to be their "living room."

But Centre 454 was itself at risk of becoming homeless, and by 2010 the search was on in earnest for a new location. Finding a site for a social service program aimed at people experiencing homelessness is not an easy business. The new location would have to be downtown somewhere, within walking distance of shelters, and with access to bus routes so that those who needed the services would be able to get there. But downtown rents are high, and city zoning bylaws are restrictive, and residents are leery, to say the least, of drawing those who are homeless into their neighbourhoods. One solution, however, kept presenting itself to the search team: why not move back to St. Albans, where the Centre had originally been located?

Centre 454 had been located in the basement of St. Albans church for 24 years, from 1976 until 2000. Even its name had been drawn from the street address of the church: 454 King Edward Avenue. It would be a homecoming of sorts. Of course, there would be complications. The space would need to be renovated. Some neighbours would be outraged, even though the centre would only be moving a distance of six city blocks, less than a kilometre from its expiring lease on Murray Street. Given the slow pace of the negotiations, no one could say for sure when the church would be available. But it soon became apparent that moving Centre 454 back to St. Albans was the best option. We had a plan for the basement.

Now all we needed was a plan for the upstairs, for the church proper. Surprisingly, this was something of an afterthought, driven as the diocese was by the urgency of Centre 454's expiring lease and by the complications and frustrations of the negotiations, which experienced delay after delay in coming to a resolution in the fall of 2010.

There is, I suppose, a certain irony in having the needs of the church become a secondary issue in all of this. Perhaps though, there was not just irony, but also a bit of divine inspiration at work. Ministry and mission became the drivers, and the vision and shape of the church which would ultimately support that ministry and mission was developed in response. It was a given that a worshipping community would have to be re-established upstairs. Not only would the absence of a congregation in one of the most historic churches in the city be unthinkable, but city bylaws required the existence of a worshipping community in the church building in order to allow its basement to be used for social services.

Many people, myself included, assumed that once we regained access to the church building, the diocese would simply engage a retired priest on a part-time basis to lead worship on Sunday mornings for whoever showed up. Some assumed that a certain remnant from the old congregation, those who wanted to remain in the Anglican Church of Canada and those who had previously scattered as a result of various disagreements, would return and form the nucleus of a renewed and re-established parish of St. Alban the Martyr. But we were wrong.

* * *

The Anglican Parish of Huntley is a three-point parish located in Carp, on the western fringes of Ottawa. If Carp is famous for anything, it is the annual Carp Fair, a three-day agricultural extravaganza with live animals and live music, with midway rides and fun for the whole family. The Carp Fair has been going strong since 1863. It is annual proof of the strong agricultural heritage that shapes the people whose village is slowly transforming into a bedroom community for those who work in Ottawa. I began serving the parish of Huntley in 2008. It was a wonderful place for a newly ordained minister to fumble his way through the beginnings of a new career. And it was the church where I met Meredith.

I heard Meredith before I saw him. There was no choir at St. James Carp when I started there; but, to my astonishment, one Sunday morning the opening hymn was supported by a strong voice singing the bass line. It didn't take long to find the voice, or voices actually, because there was also a beautiful soprano on the melody added to our vocal mix. There on my left was a new couple in church, singing with the voices of angels. Greeting them afterwards, I found out that Meredith and Barbara were indeed experienced musicians and choristers and that they had retired to the Carp area. Not long after, I also found out that they were refugees from St. Albans.

I didn't know it at the time, but that Sunday morning was the first time Meredith had set foot in an Anglican church in years. Later, as I got to know him and Barbara over wonderful meals and the occasional glass of sherry at their home, he told me pieces of his story. He had been the music director at St. Albans for a long time in the '80s and '90s.

"Was it a traditional worship style, a high-church type of liturgy?" I asked.

"More than that," he replied. "It was positively Victorian!"

But in the mid-'90s a new priest had been appointed, the one who eventually led the congregation out of the Anglican Church of

Canada in 2008. His was a strong personality, and he and Meredith clashed. Eventually Meredith left in a parting that was unpleasant to say the least.

My conversations with Meredith were happening just about the time that the St. Albans negotiations were drawing to a conclusion – before I got the call from the bishop's office, but just as the conversations about what would happen at St. Albans were heating up. So I asked what was, to me, the obvious question.

"Meredith, when our diocese starts up again at St. Albans later this year, how many people do you think are coming back?"

The answer was a bit of a surprise; at least it would have surprised the folks at our diocesan office: "No one's coming back."

It turned out that the timing was all wrong for a simple re-establishment of St. Albans. Most of the people who had issues with the direction taken by the priest appointed in the mid-'90s had left a long time ago, and they'd had plenty of time to settle into new church homes. For its part, the departing congregation was a cohesive group that had been separate from the diocese for three years and would continue to stick together. There wasn't likely to be anyone coming back. I'm not sure how many people realized it in early 2011, but St. Albans was going to be a new church plant, the creation of a new church community.

Maybe it's a good thing that no one knew. After all, the Anglican Diocese of Ottawa hadn't planted a new urban congregation in generations. Most of our experience in starting new congregations was in response to the boom days of suburban sprawl back in the '60s and '70s. But even in a fast-growing suburban area, our most recent attempt at planting a new church had gone nowhere. Church planting isn't really part of the culture of the so-called mainline churches (Anglican/Episcopal, Lutheran, Presbyterian, United, Methodist, etc.) in the way that it is for many evangelical and non-denominational churches. For us, there wasn't any playbook, and there weren't any obvious models to draw upon. It looked like we were going to have to make things up as we went along.

This is the story of that new church community.

ONE

Getting Ready

Since nobody realized that St. Albans was going to need a new congregation, nobody gave me any advice or resources about church planting. In fact, the term wasn't even really part of our Anglican vocabulary in Ottawa. We knew about something called "Fresh Expressions," a movement coming out of the U.K. that involved new forms of church and church activities. We'd heard about the "missional church," the idea that churches couldn't just sit back anymore and do what they'd always done. Instead, they should get out there and meet the needs of their neighbourhoods, taking on service and social justice initiatives as a way of building community. I'd even been to a conference on the "emerging church," the notion that there is a fundamental change taking place in Christianity in our time, and that out of this a new way of being church is emerging. But church planting – that was something more associated with evangelical and non-denominational churches than with the Anglican church. After all, we had churches just about everywhere, and lots of them were in downtown Ottawa. Many people think that we have too many downtown churches. Why would we want to plant a new one?

St. Albans would be something new, something that went against the grain of our conventional thinking and that appealed to me. I've always loved a challenge. Here was a chance to *do* and *be* church differently, to try something that might appeal to the younger demographic that was missing in many of our parishes, to be the church in a way that wasn't constricted by years of habit, tradition, and the cultural influence of previous generations. This was an exciting opportunity. But they didn't teach us any of this stuff in seminary, so it was time to do a little research.

I *did* know the story of one church plant. About ten years ago, my family and I had taken a holiday to Australia, and I had foolishly arrived at the airport for the 16-hour flight with nothing to read. So I went to the airport bookstore. As is my habit, I went straight to the bargain bin of discounted books. There in the bin, for the princely sum of six dollars, was a copy of *The Purpose-Driven Church*, by Rick Warren, the story of the beginnings of Saddleback Church in California in the 1980s. Not the sort of book that most people would pick up to read on a flight, which is probably why it was in the discount bin. But for someone about to be ordained and embarking on a new career in church ministry, it would do; and I certainly couldn't complain about the price. By the time I finished the book, somewhere between Fiji and New Zealand, the idea of planting a church was something I thought I might like to do someday. What impressed me most about Rick Warren's account were not the particulars of his understanding of church or his methodology, or Saddleback itself. Rather, it was his commitment, discipline, and ability to execute on his vision and mission. What I recognized in Rick Warren was a fellow entrepreneur at work.

In his article "Making Ministry Difficult," which appeared in *The Christian Century*, Will Willimon wrote that the most effective clergy are finding ways to start new communities of faith, but that seminaries are not teaching them how to do it. Today's ministry requires a level of entrepreneurship more easily learned in business school than in a seminary. It also requires quite a few other things that aren't taught in seminary. Digital literacy, for instance – which includes social media, email marketing, and web design – is becoming an essential skill for the newly ordained. If Willimon was right, I was off to a good start. My previous career in the technology industry had given me the entrepreneurial skills I needed. Maybe, without knowing it, I'd been preparing for the adventure of church planting for most of my life.

I'd been born into the Christian faith and the Anglican tradition. My best memories of childhood were Sundays: going to church with my family, singing in the children's choir at Christ Church Beaurepaire in Montreal, and then gathering with every relative within driving distance at my grandmother's house nearby for lunch. By the time I was eight years old, I had the entire service from the old *Book of Common Prayer* memorized, along with most of the choral settings. I knew our liturgy inside and out. Now, some might think that such familiarity with the "traditional" way of doing things would be a disadvantage for someone about to start a new congregation, and who wants to do things in new and innovative ways. I disagree.

When I was a teenager, I spent some time with classmates learning French in the south of France. During that summer, we visited a small village on the Mediterranean coast, and in that village was an even smaller museum dedicated to the work of Pablo Picasso. It contained none of the canvases or styles that one would normally associate with the famous painter. Instead, it was a collection of paintings and drawings by Picasso as a teenager. I was amazed to see that they were all in various classical styles. The teenaged Picasso painted portraits with the dark colours of Rembrandt, landscapes in the impressionist style of Monet, and still lifes using the pointillism of Seurat. The variety of artistic styles and the quality of the art was amazing, but what I took away from that experience was something else entirely. Before Picasso embarked on one of the most innovative painting careers of the 20th century, he had, as a teenager, mastered the classical styles and techniques. It's those who know a tradition inside and out who can successfully innovate and move beyond it.

My own education and professional career could also be described as eclectic. My first degree was in engineering, my second in theoretical physics, and my third in development economics, with a heavy dose of philosophy courses whenever I could fit them into my schedule. But if there was anything that served as a unifying theme, apart from the love of a good challenge, it was my fascination with models. Models, conceptual frameworks, paradigms, or, if they are comprehensive enough in scope, worldviews, are the lenses through which we understand, interpret, and interact with the world around us. Without models, engineers can't build bridges and economists would have nothing to say about economic behaviour. But the one model that captivated me more than any other and that has stayed with me as a life-long passion is the model of quantum physics.

Until my second year of university, I was immersed in the model of classical physics. Newtonian physics. Matter, motion, and forces. Causality and determinism. Objective reality. The clockwork universe. Atoms as miniature billiard balls bouncing around on a stage of space and time. But, in my second year of university, all that changed when I hit quantum physics, with a few doses of Einstein's relativity thrown in for good measure. Atoms turned out to be mostly empty space. Particles turned into waves. Waves turned into particles. An electron could be in two places at the same time. Causality and determinism both disappeared at the microscopic level. Day by day as I went to class, the common-sense ideas I'd grown up with – ideas like space, time, matter, particle, mass, causality, determinism and objectivity – all of these were chewed up and spit out, to be replaced by strange new conceptions. My brain hurt as it was forced to move from the comfortable world of classical physics to the brave new world of quantum physics, with its curving space-time, wave functions, tunneling electrons, and uncertainty principles. It's one thing to talk about paradigm shifts – it's a very different thing entirely to experience one.

Curiously enough, at the same time as I was being both disrupted and fascinated by these shifting paradigms, I discovered that Bob Brow, the priest at the Anglican church on the corner of the campus, was also a big fan of models and paradigm shifts. He would regularly incorporate these ideas into his preaching. "But what if we were to look at this with a new model," was one of his favourite ways of bringing fresh insight to a familiar passage of scripture. We would often talk at the Wednesday morning breakfasts at the church. He offered to read a paper I'd written on the wider influence of scientific models. My thesis, which I still maintain, is that the conceptual frameworks developed by scientists to explain and understand nature have a profound impact on the worldviews of society at large, and consequently affect our understanding in fields as diverse as politics, philosophy, and theology. Bob read my paper and promptly handed me a book to read: *The Structure of Scientific Revolutions* by Thomas Kuhn. This was the classic text in which Kuhn introduced the world to the idea of a "paradigm shift" using examples from the history of science. Progress and change don't happen as a result of the incremental accumulation of more and more facts. Real, substantive, ground-breaking change results from paradigm shifts: conceptual revolutions that ask new questions, fundamentally change the rules of the game, and rewrite all the textbooks.

Is the church in North America in the early 21st century in the midst of a paradigm shift? Or, to turn the question around, does the 21st-century church *need* a paradigm shift? Many would say yes. A quick survey of books and blogs inundates us with the emerging church, the converging church, the disappearing church, the post-Christendom church, the missional church, and much more. Something's happening in church-land, and there are parallels with Kuhn's analysis of the history of science. One of the parallels is surely this: paradigm shifts are generally difficult, disruptive, and divisive.

If there is a paradigm shift happening, I want to be right in the middle of it. That's what drew me to quantum physics. My thesis, among other things, explored the transition from the classical to the quantum way of understanding a particular molecular rotation. Years later, when I was lecturing on the history of science at a local college, I used to teach my students the importance of paradigm shifts. First, I would walk my students through the Copernican revolution. Since none of these 21st-century students were seriously attached to the notion that the earth must be the centre of the universe, we were able to note the dynamics of that scientific revolution in a relatively detached manner, with nothing personal at stake. Then I told them, "Now that you understand what a paradigm shift is, it's time to experience one." With that warning, we would plunge into special and general relativity and quantum physics, and over the course of about a month, we did some serious mind-blowing, much like I experienced in my university days, but without having to learn the math. My students discovered firsthand that it's one thing to learn about paradigm shifts, but it's another thing entirely to experience one. The negative side effects include headaches and confusion, but the positive effects include a profound sense of wonder, an openness to new ideas, and a useful humility about the limits of human understanding.

A colleague doing campus ministry at the University of Ottawa once asked me the single most important thing that quantum physics had taught me as far as my faith is concerned. I think it took me about a month to answer the question, but finally I told him that quantum physics had taught me to hold my ideas lightly, knowing that the concepts and words that I use actually contain more mystery, meaning, and majesty than I could ever imagine. The same applies, perhaps even more so, to our theology and ecclesiology.

I believe that we are in the midst of a paradigm shift in the church in our time and place, and that's one of the reasons that I jumped at the opportunity to plant a church in downtown Ottawa. There is room for new ways to do and be church that will change the rule book and shift our expectations. Many church leaders, in response to the challenges of our time, are burning themselves out trying to do more and to do it better, when what we *really* need are new models.

But while having a passion for shifting paradigms is a good start for a church planter, ideas alone won't get a church plant off the ground. I once had a conversation with a colleague from another denomination that was intentionally planting a lot of churches.

"How's that working?" I asked.

"Not so well," was her response. "We have a lot of good pastors out there doing good work, but most of them have no experience as entrepreneurs."

Entrepreneurs are people who make things happen. They identify and initiate new ventures, source and organize the required resources, take on risks and deal with uncertainty. We usually associate entrepreneurship with the world of business, but the same concept can apply to any new venture, and a church plant certainly falls into that category.

A couple of weeks after I got the call from the bishop about St. Albans, an email showed up in my inbox. It was from a big church in town that operated a conference centre and they were upgrading their furniture. As a result, they had plenty of used chairs to sell, and they sent out an email blast to other churches in the area to see who might be interested. I had yet to set foot in the St. Albans church building, but I had an inkling that we would want to make our space more flexible, and for that we would need chairs. Chairs at the usual price would be beyond our financial means, at least for a while. These used chairs, however, were cheap, and I knew they were in good condition, having sat on one myself at a recent synod meeting. I had no idea if the colours would match. In fact, there was a real risk that we'd never even use them. But it was too good an opportunity to pass up, so I rushed over to the church conference centre and arranged to buy 100. I managed to scrape together the $700 price I'd negotiated, and booked a cube van to take them over to a temporary storage facility. It was a risk, and I just about put my back out hauling chairs around that day. But St. Albans had its chairs, and they did indeed turn out to be a great asset, allowing us to reconfigure the church space.

In the grand scheme of things, chairs are no big deal. But their purchase illustrates what entrepreneurs do. They spot opportunities, make decisions, take risks, find resources, and make things happen.

That entrepreneurial instinct was one of the reasons that midway through my graduate studies in physics at Oxford I decided that I didn't want to pursue academia. I decided, instead, to put my engineering background to use in international development, with the goal of adapting technologies for use in developing countries. I started working for a technology company based in Ottawa doing projects around the world in solar energy and rural telecommunications. It was the perfect place to learn how to be an entrepreneur. When I started, we had ten employees. By the time I resigned as CEO, we had over 100 employees, we'd spun out a start-up Internet company, and we'd made a major strategic shift from rural telecom to air traffic management as our core business. We enjoyed huge successes, including recognition as one of Canada's fastest-growing businesses. *And* we had some huge flops, including the failure of our Internet start-up after the dot-com bubble burst in 2001.

By then I was ready for a change. Too much business travel was taking its toll, both on me and on my growing family. It was time to consider other options. I took a sabbatical from work and started thinking about a second career. I also seized the opportunity to do a lot of things that I had never found time for during the previous decade – piano lessons, cycling, coaching children's hockey and soccer, writing, working with the teens at church. People often ask me how it came about that I shifted from business and engineering to ordained ministry. It wasn't part of any grand plan, at least on my part. I'm afraid I have no story of blinding insight or dramatic change to tell them. I just started trying different things during my sabbatical, and when something resonated, I kept on doing it. One of the things that resonated during that year was theology. I took a theology course at the local university, and something clicked, so I took another.

At the time, I wasn't sure what would come next, but perhaps God would find a use for a slightly-burned-out, 40-year-old quantum physicist turned entrepreneur with a passion for shifting paradigms.

Like I said, without realizing it, I had been getting ready for the St. Albans church plant for years.

TWO

The Age of Authenticity

The headline of the December 2011 issue of Toronto Life magazine tells an all-too-familiar story: "Condominium: $1 Million for the Coolest Converted-Church Condo We've Seen Yet."

We live in an age in which we are more likely to hear about a converted-church condominium downtown than a new urban church plant. Declining attendance figures, flight to the suburbs, changing urban demographics, the growth of the "nones" (those who claim "no church affiliation" on census forms) – all have contributed to the conventional wisdom in church circles that we have too many downtown churches.

Perhaps that explains why, when my appointment to St. Albans was announced, the first email I received from one of my colleagues had the subject line "Congratulations, I think." There soon followed others whose common theme was "I'll pray for you." The tone wasn't unexpected. Those of us who hang out in church circles are only too familiar with the narrative of decline that has insinuated itself over the last 30 years or more.

In my own denomination, the Anglican Church of Canada, membership has dropped from a peak of 1.35 million Canadians in 1961, to about 500,000 by 2011. In my Diocese of Ottawa, we hired a consultant in 2006 to assess our particular situation, and the message that came back wasn't pretty: time to look at closing churches and consolidating urban parishes. It wasn't a popular message. But it *did* reflect the trends both locally and nationally.

The Pew Research Center's study *Canada's Changing Religious Landscape* was published in 2013. The study uses Canadian census data to illustrate what it calls the big trends in religious life in Canada: disaffiliation and decline in attendance. Disaffiliation began to rise in Canada in the 1970s. In 1971, only 4% of Canadians did not declare a religious affiliation (the "nones") in response to census surveys. By 2011, that figure had increased six-fold to 24%. Decline in attendance mirrors the drop in affiliation. Way back in the post-war era, Canada had an exceptionally high rate of religious attendance, peaking at around 60% weekly in 1950.

I have fond memories of Sunday mornings from my childhood. No alarm clocks, no school, a cooked breakfast, and going to church with my mom, dad, and brother. Afterwards, we'd all gather for Sunday lunch, and then watch the hockey or football game. It was a weekly ritual, a special time set apart from the rest of the week. Most people in our neighbourhood did the same. Not everyone went to church, but everyone seemed to enjoy that special day of the week, which had been carved out as a time apart from work and programmed activities.

But those Sunday mornings are gone. Gradually, the space that had been set aside for church and family on Sunday mornings in our culture has been eroded. At some point over the last 40 years, we reached what author Malcolm Gladwell calls the "tipping point." Sundays became the same as Saturdays for most people. Now, even the distinction between weekday and weekend is starting to fade. The time that had been set apart on Sunday mornings became a window of opportunity for a whole variety of other activities. Sunday shopping began. Minor sports teams snapped up the ice time and the gym space. More and more people either elected or were obliged to work. At last count, more than one-third of employed Americans work on a typical weekend day.

For those of us who still want to go to church on Sundays, that can be a challenge. We have to maneuver around work schedules and appointments. We often travel on weekends. If we have children, it gets even more complicated. Soccer practice, hockey games, birthday parties, the list goes on. And when we do make it to church on a Sunday morning, it's often our friends who are absent because of an activity or a weekend work shift, so we don't get to see them as we had hoped. Because of all these competing interests and time pressures, many people who consider themselves regular churchgoers are now more likely to attend once or twice a month rather than weekly.

Going to church was the thing to do in the 1950s. But as the years passed, Sunday mornings became more crowded with alternative activities, and churches became less crowded. In 1975, 42% of Canadians attended religious services at least once a month. By 2010, even that figure had dropped to 28%, with most of the decline happening in the 1980s and 1990s. And Canada is not unique. The same trends became apparent even earlier in Europe.

While it was once thought that the United States was an exception, it turns out that in the U.S.A. there was simply a delay; the number of religiously-unaffiliated adults, which had remained relatively stable throughout the '70s and '80s began to rise in the 1990s, going from 8% in 1990 to 23% by 2014. Weekly or more religious attendance appears to have fallen from the relatively stable level of around 40% that was seen in the late 20th century to levels of either 36% or 31% by 2013, depending on whether you believe the telephone or the online version of the survey. The reliability of these statistics and the reasons for the decline have become hot topics on the American religious scene recently. It looks like there are no exceptions after all in the Western industrialized world.

The narrative of decline is well-grounded in both anecdotal evidence and statistics. To many observers, it appeared that the secular hypothesis of social theorists such as Marx, Weber, and Durkheim was being proven correct. Religion would eventually disappear in the face of modernization, science, and the advance of society. As

Reginald Bibby, the leading sociologist of religious trends in Canada put it, "people observing the Canadian scene between 1960 and 2000 were virtually unanimous in viewing organized religion as being in irreversible decline." Who in their right mind would start a new church in urban Ottawa in 2011?

But the secular hypothesis, that religion will inevitably disappear, has come under attack over the past two decades. The enduring vitality of religion in the 21st century has defied the expectations of many secularists. Sociologist Peter Berger wrote in 1996 that, on the contrary, no one should have been surprised by the vitality of religious groups throughout the world, because human beings are by nature religious. "The religious impulse, the quest for meaning that transcends the restricted space of empirical existence in this world, has been a perennial feature of humanity." So if the theory of religious decline as inevitable and irreversible is not sufficient to explain what we've been witnessing, how can we improve our understanding of the trends of the last 50 years in order to get a better grip on our current situation?

Perhaps the person who has put the most thought into this is Canadian philosopher Charles Taylor, whose monumental work *A Secular Age* was published in 2007. In *A Secular Age*, Taylor takes on the secular hypothesis that religion will inevitably disappear. It is, Taylor would argue, a theory that is erroneously fuelled by simplistic subtraction stories. Taylor readily recognizes that we are indeed living in a secular age. But he rejects the easy answer for why this has come about. The secularists' easy answer is that modernity brings about secularity, and they usually explain this by way of subtraction stories: human beings have discarded or have liberated themselves from the illusions and limitations in knowledge that characterized previous ages. The most common subtraction story involves science, the idea that modern science, by providing explanations for things that once were explained by religion, succeeds in crowding out belief, and that this movement is both inevitable and irreversible. But Taylor argues that these subtraction stories are a distortion of what actually took place. "A common 'subtraction' story attributes everything to disenchantment," he says. "First science gave us 'naturalistic' explanations of the world. And then people began to look for alternatives to God. But things didn't work that way." Subtraction stories are neither cogent, nor adequate, nor historically accurate. As is often the case in the study of social history, the better explanation is both more complex and more subtle. What Taylor argues in great detail is that over the course of 500 years or more, a complex web of social, political, and economic forces have succeeded in shifting what he calls the "social imaginary," and this in turn has resulted in a change in the conditions of belief in what we commonly call the Western industrialized world.

We live in a secular age. Some people writing within the Christian tradition call this post-Christendom. But what do we mean when we identify the present age as secular? Some have in mind an understanding of how public space has changed, how one can engage in public activity without encountering God. They may refer to the way in which political organization is no longer connected to faith as it once was, say, in 16th-century Europe. Others have in mind the falling off of religious practice and belief as demonstrated by the statistics that have been cited already. But according to Taylor, we should understand the present secular age as one in which the conditions of belief have changed. We have moved from a society in which belief in God was unchallenged and unproblematic, to one in which it is understood as one option among others, and frequently not the easiest to embrace. Or as Taylor puts it succinctly, "Belief in God is no longer axiomatic. There are alternatives."

The critical moment in this transition, at least for most of Western Europe and North America, was the 1960s. That shouldn't come as a shock. The 1960s saw the birth of rock music, the sexual revolution, hippies, flower power, the growth of individualism, consumer culture, and much more. Taylor identifies the post-'60s era as the "Age of Authenticity," a time of expressive individualism in which the search for an authentic way of living takes centre stage and becomes a mass phenomenon. The 1960s marked the beginning of this great transformation. A traditional ethic of community service and self-discipline gave way to a contemporary ethic of authenticity and self-expression. Individuals were expected to find their own path in life and their own way of realizing their humanity, rather than "surrendering to conformity with a model imposed on us from outside, by society, or the previous generation, or religious or political authority."

What Taylor identifies in aggregate was lived experience for many who came of age in the '60s and '70s. Well-known author and preacher Barbara Brown Taylor is an example of one who has reflected on her own experience of this time of transformation:

As best as I can figure, the Christian era ended during my lifetime. When I was eight years old in small-town Alabama, there was nothing to do on Sundays but go to church... By the time I reached high school, God was dead. Pictures of Kent State and the My Lai massacre were tattooed on people's minds, and they turned their outrage on what they had been taught about God. God was not good. God did not answer prayer. God, for all practical purposes, was dead. All bets were off. Human beings were free to construct their own realities from any materials at hand and to express themselves any way they pleased... Organized religion remained one of the many choices available to human beings in their search for meaning, but it remained a lame one. On the college campus where I spent the early seventies, my peers let me know that only the unimaginative still went to church – the stuck, the fearful, the socially inept – while those with any sense committed themselves to more relevant causes, like the anti-war movement, or the environment, or the arts.

The world had changed, and Christianity was no longer the default option.

The move from a society in which duty and authority are the moral imperatives to one in which freedom and authenticity are normative has profound implications. The cultural imperative to "do your own thing" and the ready availability and acceptability of alternatives to religious belief have shifted the social context for religion over the last 50 years. For a church that was strongly shaped by the relative stability of religious organization in the West from 1800 to 1950, and that reached new heights of attendance and cultural influence in the 1950s, the "Age of Authenticity" has come as a rude awakening. The conditions of belief in our society have been profoundly changed.

The numbers bear this out. We have already looked at the statistics for disaffiliation and declining attendance that affect the church in Canada. But a closer look at the numbers reveals that generationally, one age cohort is primarily responsible for these trends: the baby boomers, those born in Canada between 1945 and 1965. With the benefit of hindsight, this makes sense. Given the major transformations that began in the 1960s, it is only natural, as Taylor points out, that "the generations which have been formed in the cultural revolution of the 1960s are in some respect deeply alienated from a strong traditional model of Christian faith in the West." As these alienated boomers dropped out of churches, the overall numbers dropped, and continued dropping from 1960 to 2000 in Canada. By the turn of the century, it looked like proponents of the secularization hypothesis had been proven correct.

But then a funny thing happened, at least in Canada. Around 2000, the numbers levelled off. Monthly religious attendance has been roughly stable since the year 2000. In my own province of Ontario, there were more people who attended religious services monthly in 2011 than there were in the year 2000, though it must be said that many of these make their spiritual homes in mosques and immigrant churches and not in traditional Christian denominations. While attendance among boomers remains low nationally in Canada (18% weekly in 2005), the next generation, the "post-boomers," is actually more involved (24% weekly in 2005). When pollsters move beyond the statistics of attendance and affiliation and start probing more deeply, they find that the importance of spiritual beliefs and practices in the lives of most Canadians continues to be strong. A majority of Canadians, 65%, believe that religious and spiritual beliefs are important to the way they live their lives, and 50% continue to engage in religious or spiritual practices at least monthly. Those who are concerned about religious attendance may be encouraged to know that in addition to the 28% of adult Canadians who attend religious services monthly, of the rest, fully 62% are receptive to greater involvement "if they can find it to be worthwhile."

Religion is not disappearing in North America. Churches, mosques, synagogues, and temples are not going away, and faith and spirituality will continue to be important for large numbers of Canadians and Americans. But we are operating in a changed context. We are living in an age in which duty and authority have given way to freedom and authenticity, in which deference has been replaced by discernment. We are living in an age in which spirituality is a quest that isn't necessarily embedded in a religious institution, and potential engagement with these institutions will be evaluated to determine whether it is indeed worthwhile in the context of how one's own faith journey is understood. We are living in an age in which the context for belief has changed. Belief in God is no longer axiomatic, and because there are alternatives, even those who *do* believe do so in a condition of doubt and uncertainty. This has a critical impact on the lived experience of faith. We are living in an age in which churches that have been shaped and dominated by pre-boomers are going to have to respond to the questions and needs of post-boomers, or they will disappear.

Not only is it possible to start new churches in this changed context, it is essential that we do so, for the health of the larger church and for the faith journeys of countless people who are looking at their options in the search for a spiritual home.

THREE

The Neighbourhood Battle

My first public event as the newly appointed pastor of St. Albans Church was a community meeting organized by our local city councillor to discuss the relocation of Centre 454 to St. Albans. Did I say "discuss"? Perhaps that's not an entirely accurate characterization. Indeed, the highlight of the evening was a heated exchange between the councillor and one of the local residents. The resident wanted the reluctant young councillor to watch a video of two people having sex on her front steps, as an illustration of what would happen if Centre 454 was allowed to move into the neighbourhood.

When the news broke that Centre 454 was to move back to St. Albans Church in the Sandy Hill neighbourhood, residents, local business owners, and condominium developers reacted with outrage. Fuelled by misinformation, and in some cases disinformation, people brought forth all sorts of concerns about personal safety, discarded needles, property values, drug use, and the potential for antisocial and illegal activities. Much of the anger was stoked by bad experiences that residents had had in the past with people who lived on the streets and in homeless shelters.

There's no disputing that there are homeless people in our neighbourhood. The Ottawa Mission has operated a shelter for homeless
men on our street since 1906, and there are two other large shelters
within easy walking distance. Homelessness is a serious problem,
with over 1,000 people living in shelters in Ottawa on any given night.
Affordable housing is in short supply, with upwards of 10,000 people on the city of Ottawa's waiting list. More affordable housing in
the city would certainly help. But housing alone won't solve the problem of homelessness. According to Diane Morrison, executive director of The Ottawa Mission at the time, providing affordable housing
to the chronically homeless is of limited value:

These are people who have come from a harder place. A shelter is a
scary place but the people in there have run out of options. They are
often mentally ill or have an addiction and they're often not allowed
to go back home. The chronically homeless have lived in shelters for
so long you can't just put them in a place where they have nobody to
talk to or nobody to eat with. At least shelters give them that. So
once they are housed, what resources are you going to give them?
You can't just put them in a building without support.

Homelessness is a complex issue with many root causes. Certainly
one of the principle contributing factors in Ottawa and elsewhere
has been deinstitutionalization. Mental health institutions have been
closed, and those people who would formerly have been patients
and residents of these institutions are now expected to live in the
community. This process began as early as the 1960s, but was accel-
erated in Ontario in the late 1990s. Though one can argue the merits
of deinstitutionalization, the closure of psychiatric hospital beds in
the province of Ontario and the failure to put proper community
supports in place has resulted in homelessness for a large number of
people suffering from poor mental health. These are people who require support, both medical and non-medical, in order to stabilize
their lives. On any given night in Ottawa, many of them will be sleeping in our neighbourhood, in one of the local shelters.

The second contributing factor to homelessness identified by Morrison is addiction. People on the street and in shelters have run out of options and they are vulnerable to addiction. Some turn to drug and alcohol abuse because they are on the street; some are on the street because of their drug and alcohol abuse. It's a vicious circle. In Ottawa, the problem of substance abuse took a turn for the worse when crack cocaine hit the streets in 2005. Crack offers a quick high, is very addictive, and is relatively cheap, which means that even the poor become targets for dealers. More users and more addictions result in broken lives and greater security concerns. It becomes much more difficult for those working in shelters and other social services to create a safe and healthy environment for those who use their services.

Recently, we've become more aware of a third factor that gives rise to homelessness and shelter use. Over the last few years, I've noticed as I listened to homeless people tell their stories that they would often mention something about a head injury: a car accident, a blow to the head, a sport-related concussion. In the past few years, this anecdotal evidence has been confirmed by researchers. Traumatic brain injury is a major factor in homelessness. As noted by Angela Chapin in an article in *The Ottawa Citizen* on May 31, 2014, a recent study by St. Michael's Hospital in Toronto confirmed that almost half of homeless men had suffered a traumatic brain injury, and that 87% of those injuries happened before the men lost their homes. It turns out that among the reasons some people end up homeless and living in shelters is the concussion they sustained playing hockey, or the car accident that resulted in a blow to the head.

This rang true for me when I suffered my own concussion a couple of years ago while playing soccer. It kept me out of sports for over a year, and even today symptoms persist. My concussion was mild compared to many incidents of traumatic brain injury. But even so, in the immediate aftermath of the concussion, my focus and stamina waned and my mood deteriorated. As a result, I was less effective in my work and I was irritable in my relationships. I was fortunate, though; I was able to keep my job, and my family stood by me despite my grouchiness. But for many who sustain injuries far worse than mine or whose support networks are thin, the result can be loss of employment, broken relationships, and time spent in a homeless shelter. We are also becoming aware that the same can be said for many who suffer from post-traumatic stress disorder.

So yes, homelessness is a big problem in our city. It represents, in fact, a whole cluster of problems, including poverty, unemployment, mental illness, addictions, traumatic brain injury, chronic disease, family breakdown, lack of affordable housing, and the list goes on. Homelessness is, first and foremost, a tragedy for those who are homeless. It also has an impact on the neighbourhood and its residents.

But day programs such as Centre 454 are part of the solution, not the problem. Day programs provide support for the poor and homeless who are already living in the neighbourhood, in shelters and in low-income housing. These programs actually get people *off* the streets by providing them with a safe place to go during the day, giving them a sense of community and putting them in contact with vital services that they can use to stabilize and transform their lives. At Centre 454, these support services include mental and physical health care, counselling, and literacy programs. The Centre provides professional help with issues such as housing, addictions, and employment, and offers social recreation and practical supports like laundry and shower facilities.

But there was no telling that to the people who streamed into the first public meeting at the Sandy Hill Community Centre. Within days of the announcement that the diocese was planning to move Centre 454 back to St. Albans, opponents in the neighbourhood went to the media. In an effort to create a forum for dialogue, the local community association invited representatives of the Anglican Diocese and of Centre 454 to their next scheduled meeting so that they could respond to any questions that might come up. But the organizers had no idea what was about to transpire. The meeting room was standing-room-only and the meeting itself was a free-for-all. It was as if all of the anger that had been bottled up in the community over drug use, illegal activity, street violence, panhandling, garbage, trespassing and the like, exploded, with Centre 454 as the flashpoint.

And while most people expressed sincere concerns, and many genuinely wanted to get more information about the Centre and its planned move, there were other voices who said some degrading things about those experiencing homelessness, many of whom were actually in the room, listening in silence. Ill-advised comments resulted in anger on both sides and the war of words escalated. When a journalist called the next day, a diocesan official, upset with suggestions that the homeless be simply "carted away," reacted by saying that it sounded like Nazi Germany. That made the headlines! Local residents became even more outraged. More meetings followed, tempers flared, the most strident of the neighbours formed an association and hired lawyers, and leaflets opposing the relocation of Centre 454 were distributed around the neighbourhood. I distinctly remember one of the residents coming up to me afterwards and saying, with more than a hint of sarcasm, "Good luck starting a new congregation in a neighbourhood where everybody hates you."

But opponents of Centre 454 underestimated the church's resolve and overestimated their own legal position. For the church and for me, support for Centre 454 was a gospel imperative. We are called to stand with the poor and the oppressed in our society. Moving Centre 454 back into the basement of St. Albans Church was the best way to serve those who needed the Centre's services, and so we stood firm, knowing that we were doing as best we could the work that Jesus had called us to do.

But at the same time that we resolved to stand for the poor in our midst, we also wanted to be good neighbours. That verse about "loving your neighbour" is also a gospel imperative. It wasn't easy and it certainly wasn't comfortable. It was particularly difficult for the executive director of Centre 454, who was on the receiving end of most of the derogatory emails. But we swallowed our anger and continued to engage with our neighbours, listening to their concerns, coming up with action plans to address potential problems, working with partners such as city officials and the police to address issues that were outside our control. In response to the outcry from local residents, our city councillor set up a neighbourhood group that would meet regularly and act as a forum for dealing with potential problems as they arose. We made information available and slowly corrected piece by piece and person by person the misinformation about the Centre and its programs that continued to swirl around the neighbourhood.

It was tempting in the midst of all the anger and emotional turmoil to feel that everyone was against us. But that was hardly the case. Many in the neighbourhood valued the services provided by Centre 454. The church was there for us, from the folks in the pews to the bishop himself, validating the work we were doing, offering advice and comfort, and supporting us in prayer. The City of Ottawa was quick to affirm its support for the work of Centre 454 and to make clear that the move to the basement of St. Albans was in accordance with zoning bylaws, as long as the church had a worshipping congregation. Of course, some of the opponents were quick to jump on that particular clause and cast doubt on our ability to re-establish a congregation at St. Albans.

Individuals came forward and offered support. I remember one woman in particular, a senior living in the neighbourhood, who showed up at one of our first church services. "I live just a few blocks from here," she told me, "and I received in my mailbox this leaflet saying all sorts of terrible things about St. Albans Church and Centre 454. And when I saw the way they were badmouthing an organization that was just trying to do some good and help the poor in our neighbourhood, I decided that I better come and worship here to show my support." She still worships with us today.

One of the challenges in those early days of 2011 was that even though we were convinced that Centre 454 would be an asset for the neighbourhood, the actual move-in date for the Centre to St.

Albans was still over a year away. We wouldn't even have access to the building for several months, and after that a major renovation would be required to adapt the space for the Centre's needs. Some residents were making wild claims about the wave of crime that would sweep the neighbourhood when Centre 454 moved in, assertions which we knew were unfounded, but couldn't be definitively put to rest. In the meantime, opponents of the move were contacting lawyers and lobbying the city to have the funding for Centre 454 revoked. It was all quite disheartening for the staff and participants of the Centre. Something to boost morale was definitely in order.

Every year, the Community Ministries of the Anglican Diocese of Ottawa holds what we call our "Annual Celebration." The Annual Celebration is a bit like an Annual General Meeting, but a lot more fun. Community Ministries consists of five service organizations. Three of them, Centre 454, The Well, and St. Luke's Table are day programs serving those who are homeless and vulnerable in our city. Cornerstone Housing for Women operates the downtown women's emergency shelter in Ottawa and provides supportive housing for women. The Ottawa Pastoral Counselling Centre offers individual, couple, and family counselling. Each year we hold our Annual Cele-bration, an opportunity to hear more about the work of these ministries and to learn about the people who are involved in them through poetry, music, and drama. The Annual Celebration is attended by staff, volunteers, and participants, as well as by supporters in the church and the community. We usually invite a guest speaker, someone we want to honour for his or her work in supporting the vulnerable and those in need in our community. As the chair of the Community Ministries Committee in 2011, right in the middle of the Centre 454 controversy, I suggested that we should invite Mayor Jim Watson.

It was a good time to invite the mayor. The City of Ottawa had just passed its 2011 budget, which included a new 14-million-dollar annual commitment to reducing homelessness and to increasing affordable housing, something that the Anglican Church and the Community Ministries had pushed hard for in the 2010 municipal elections. This would be an opportunity to express our thanks for that, and of course to advocate for continued action. But it was also an opportunity for all of us and especially for the staff, volunteers and participants of Centre 454 to hear straight from the mayor what he had to say about the move back to St. Albans. What he said, in a nutshell, was this: "I've got your backs." He talked about how valuable the work of the church was in providing services to the poor and vulnerable in our community. He talked about his personal commitment and the commitment of the city to reducing chronic homelessness. And he thanked us for the work of Centre 454 and all of our Community Ministries, and confirmed that the move of Centre 454 to St. Albans was supported by the city and by city staff in its social services department. It was welcome news, and I think that, after that evening, all of us who had been involved in the neighbourhood controversy started to breathe just a little bit easier.

As it turned out, moving Centre 454 back to St. Albans took much longer than planned. It isn't easy to renovate a 145-year-old building! After various surprises and delays, we were finally ready for the Centre to make the move in November 2012, 21 months after the initial announcement. I was both nervous and excited at the same time. Excited, because the reopening of the Centre was the result of many months' work and because it would have a big impact on our nascent church community; nervous, because I knew that some of the neighbours were still watching and would jump on anything that went wrong. My greatest fear was that a random event, a theft or a mugging, would happen on the street just after the Centre reopened and that it would be seized on as an example of the crime wave that had been unleashed. But there was nothing of the sort. The Centre moved back into St. Albans, programs restarted, and the fears of our neighbours began to recede. Much of the credit is due to the staff and participants of the Centre. Every day, staff walk the block morning, noon, and afternoon, just to make sure everything is all right, and to provide a little guidance to anyone on the street who

might need it. Neighbours were invited in for an open house, and
the Centre staff worked closely with city officials, police, resident
associations, and neighbouring service providers to ensure a smooth
transition.

What took many of us by surprise, however, was the extent to
which participants were impacted by the move to the church. Even
though the Centre has its own space in the basement of St. Albans
with its own set of entrance doors, participants as well as staff and
volunteers would often comment on how good it felt to be at the
church. Perhaps it's the peaceful church garden that is now part of
Centre 454, an oasis of green in the midst of asphalt and concrete.
Perhaps it is the beautiful architecture of the church itself, an inspiring neo-Gothic stone building now dwarfed by high-rise condo-
miniums. But most importantly, judging by the comments I've heard,
participants understand that the church is a sanctuary, a good place,
even a sacred place where they are welcome.

The neighbourhood fears about the consequences of the move
of Centre 454 to St. Albans did not materialize. That's not to say
that homelessness and poverty aren't a concern in our neighbourhood; they still are. There are still concerns about drugs and needles, crime and anti-social behaviour (although according to police
and city officials, the incidence of such things on our street has
virtually disappeared). But in all, I think we've managed to dem-
onstrate that Centre 454 is part of the solution, not part of the
problem. About a year after the move, I dropped into the sales
office of the new condominium that backs onto St. Albans. I'd been
invited by one of the members of the condo board to drop off some
posters for a play that we were hosting. That in itself was a good
sign. As I entered the condo office, there was a sales representative for the condo developer behind the desk. I introduced myself,
we chatted for a moment, and he agreed to deliver the envelope
for me. And then, just as I was turning to leave, he said, "You know,
I was an opponent when I first found out about what you guys
were doing. I thought it would cause all sorts of problems. But I've

changed my mind. I think some of our fears were misplaced."

Then he added, "I thought it would be impossible to sell the units which backed onto your property. But now I point out to people that if they purchase one of those condos they'll get a view of your beautiful church. It's become a sales feature!"

FOUR

Launch on Facebook, Meet in the Pub

A church plant opens up the possibility of doing and being church differently. A quick look around any North American city like Ottawa reveals a hundred different ways of being church, but most of them are variations on a few themes. St. Albans was a chance to do some exploration, to try something new, free from pastoral concerns about the effects of change on existing members and without the default position of "we've always done it this way." There was little to be gained in duplicating models that were already being done well in our city. We needed to find our own model. We needed to articulate a new vision and to build a narrative to support it. And we needed to do it quickly.

I was facing a steep learning curve. A colleague mentioned that the Anglican Diocese of Toronto, the "big diocese" across the province from us, had developed a manual for church planting. I searched on their website and there it was, a working draft, but available for download nonetheless. So I started reading. It was a thick document, 84 pages in total, and it included some good stuff about the type of leadership required for church planting, building a team, setting up a communications plan, focusing on the vision for mission and ministry, and so on. But the one thing that got my attention more than anything else was the timeline for planning a church plant, which I found on page 30. Working backwards from the day of the first public worship service were all the things that you were supposed to do as part of your preparation: two months prior, prepare launch team for grand opening; 4 months prior, set date for grand opening, massive publicity begins; six months prior, seek musicians and other worship leaders; all the way to 48 months out, leader calls for a new church, visioning group forms long-range action plan. It was incredibly thorough and well laid out. There was only one problem. The date for the first public worship service for the new St. Albans had already been set. We didn't have four years to get ready; we had three months.

One thing that is immediately apparent to anyone looking at the mainline churches in North America is that, in many of them, there is a demographic gap. The missing demographic is young adults, or "millennials," to use the language created by demographers. Our churches, formed as many of them were during the boom days of the 1950s and '60s, have a disproportionate number of people who came of age during that same era. Perhaps that's to be expected. What did come as more of a surprise to me is that when I started scratching beneath the surface, I discovered that many of the absent millennials were missing in action not because they were simply disinterested or had given up on religion, but because they felt alienated and even marginalized by our church culture. They didn't feel welcome, and they didn't belong. Going to church for some had become too much of a cultural commute. St. Albans would have to find a way to shorten that distance.

It's important for a church community to seek to incarnate itself in its local area. We didn't want St. Albans to be a drive-in church; we wanted to be a church that was rooted in the neighbourhood, a parish church in the true sense of the word. I knew the area. I'd worked here, my children had attended the local school and played hockey and ringette at the neighbourhood rink; my wife and I both had degrees from the local universities and we lived just a few kilometres away from the church building.

St. Albans is located in the midst of an awesome downtown neighbourhood: urban, diverse, growing, and pulsing with energy. A quick walkabout in the vicinity of the church in the spring of 2011 affirmed what I already knew. Within a few blocks, there are three shelters for people who are homeless, as well as the University of Ottawa with its 40,000 students. New condos were being built on every side, competing for space with rooming houses, student residences, and lovely old homes. A study of the census data confirmed what was readily apparent on the street: our census area had a high concentration of young adults. We would have to engage with their culture. We'd been handed a church building in a contemporary urban neighbourhood. We would become a contemporary urban church.

It didn't take long to figure out that social justice was going to be one of our priorities. With a day program for people who are homeless in our basement and some of the city's most vulnerable on our doorstep, service to those who are poor and marginalized was a big part of who we wanted to become. As one of our planning team members later put it, "social justice is in our DNA." But we wanted to be more than just another social service agency. We wanted our service and our thirst for social justice to be an expression of who we were as followers of Jesus. He was, after all, the one who urged his followers to feed the hungry, welcome the stranger, and care for the sick. It was important for us, first and foremost, to be Christ-centred, allowing our service to the neighbourhood and our passion for social justice to flow out of our identity as followers of Christ.

A vision for our new community began to emerge with surprising speed. As we walked and as we talked, neighbourhood characteristics coalesced with the longing of young adults for new ways of being church. Local demographics dovetailed with my own passion for student ministry. The needs of the neighbourhood, the proximity to the university, the call to social justice, and the connection with Centre 454 all stared us in the face. In the space of a few weeks in the spring of 2011, out of our prayers, reflections, and Spirit-led conversations, a vision emerged with both speed and clarity. We were going to be a "Spirit-led, Christ-centred, contemporary urban church."

Initially, those words functioned as a stick in the ground, a marker for the direction we thought we might head in. Over time, as that tag line served as a starting point for discussion and a catalyst for dreaming, the words blossomed into a vision that resonated with our nascent community. It was a statement specific and concrete enough to mean something to those who heard it, but sufficiently open that people could allow their own imaginations and perspectives to flesh it out.

"What do you think of 'Spirit-led, Christ-centred, contemporary urban church'?" I asked Andrew and Ericka over supper at their home in early April. That dinner was an important step in building the team we needed to launch our project. Andrew was the youth and young-adult missioner for the diocese. Bishop John had suggested to me that he and Ericka might want to join the visioning team for St. Albans and become part of the new congregation. They did, and over the next few days the three of us put our heads together.

We needed to build a team and we needed to craft a story and we needed to get that story out. So we made some quick decisions. The rebirth of St. Albans was a story of resurrection and new life, so what better time to make our announcement than on Easter Sunday. That meant our public launch was less than a month away. It wasn't enough time, but the story and the symbolism were too good to pass up, so we decided to do it anyway.

That led to a second decision: the launch would take place on Facebook. If we wanted to be a contemporary urban church, with a focus on ministry to young adults, then we had to go where we would find young adults, and in 2011 that meant a virtual launch on Facebook. But what were we going to launch? Sure, we could let people know that we were launching a new community, a "Spirit-Led, Christ-Centred, Contemporary Urban Church," and that our first worship service would be on July 3. We also started planning for regular Facebook posts that would allow us to create a virtual congregation in advance of that date. But there was an immediate need to build a team and to start meeting.

That led to the third decision: weekly meetings would begin on Wednesday evenings at the local pub for anyone who wanted to be involved in the launch of this new church. Doing this by way of a public announcement was a bit of a gamble. We could have built our initial team by invitation only. Opening the invitation to all and sundry was bound to lead to a more diverse assortment of people with differing aspirations as to what they might like to see in a new church. Some might say it was a recipe for disaster. But we were committed to being Spirit-led, and this seemed like an initial opportunity to put some trust in that commitment, and to see what sort of Spirit-led church might start to emerge.

With those initial decisions behind us, there was now considerable work to be done. We needed a logo, we needed a web domain, we needed Facebook, Twitter, and YouTube accounts. We needed a Facebook page and a website with a splash page to direct people to Facebook. We set up an email campaign to alert people to the launch, with everything timed to be released overnight on April 23 as folks were celebrating the Easter Vigil. We decided that a welcome video would be the best way to introduce people to our story. A script was written, filming was done, audio was recorded, and all the bits and pieces were spliced and edited. It was a lot of work and there was little money available for professional help, but Andrew is a talented guy and we managed to pull it off in time for our virtual launch on Easter Sunday, 2011.

But even as we were getting the communications materials ready, there were other tasks to be done. Andrew and Ericka connected me with a couple of their friends. One had been involved with previous church plants, another was a musician. Both had experienced the same difficulty plugging into a local church and were ready for something new. They were in. A few people started sending me emails with nibbles of interest about being part of the launch. We talked. A team started to come together. Some of the early interest, as one might expect, came from people in other Anglican parishes around town who had heard the news about St. Albans. That posed a bit of a dilemma. I remember sitting down with my archdeacon, the senior priest in the area, to talk about it.

"Peter, I don't think my colleagues will be too happy if some of their parishioners leave to join St. Albans."

"That's not your problem," he replied. "You need some good people to get off the ground. But don't let them leave where they are by the back door. If they want to join St. Albans, they should go as missionaries. Bless 'em and send 'em, the same way we would if they were going halfway around the world."

It was good advice, and over the course of the next few months three parishes of our diocese (St. John's, Ascension, and St. Michael's) did just that, blessing and sending several of their key people as missionaries to help launch our church plant. They formed the core of our launch team, and those "sending parishes" held us in prayer during our first few months and beyond.

Communications and team building were at the forefront of initial activities. But there was also important behind-the-scenes work that had to be done. Many church plants stumble before they get to financial self-sufficiency. To minimize that risk, it's important to get the financial structure right and to open good lines of communication with financial sponsors. In our case, the diocese would foot the initial bills, and it wasn't as if it was flush with cash. As is the case with most churches, budgeting is always a challenge. So once more I sat down with Bishop John, and this time the financial director of the diocese was present.

We met just as our launch team was starting to come together. These people would devote considerable time, energy, and ideas to St. Albans over the coming months, while juggling the demands of work and family life. I needed to free up some time for St. Albans, too. I had been appointed the new priest, but that wouldn't officially take effect for three months, and in the meantime I still had full-time responsibilities with the three churches in the Parish of Huntley in Carp. Like the rest of our core group, I was quite happy to put in whatever hours were needed to look after Huntley and to launch the new St. Albans, but there are limits, and it's best to put some structure around such things. So we worked out an arrangement that nominally had me working 60% of my time with the Parish of Huntley and the rest with St. Albans for the transition period. This, in turn, allowed the folks in Carp to increase the hours of their associate priest to balance things out. My St. Albans' time, initially at 40% and then full time, would be paid by the diocese for the balance of 2011, as would the costs of the St. Albans building. But that's where we drew the line. For anything else, we would have to raise the money ourselves.

At first glance, it seemed a challenge. After all, there were only six of us committed to St. Albans at the time of that meeting, with no significant financial resources to draw on. An alternative would have been for our sponsor, the diocese in this case, to commit to paying all the bills, control the spending, and take back whatever funds our community could raise to apply against the overall cost. But that would have been disastrous. That scenario would have meant that each additional dollar donated by future members of the church plant would actually funnel its way back to the diocese rather than stay in our own community. It's not that the diocese wouldn't still be offering generous support under such an arrangement, it would. But creating a financial structure in which donations at the margin benefit the sponsor rather than the church plant would seriously hamper the ability of the plant to raise money. It turned out to be much better for us to cap the diocesan contribution at a fixed amount, declining each year, so that dollars raised in our community stayed within the community and could be used to support our ministry and mission in a highly visible way.

This financial structure, as well as a host of other logistical arrangements – accounting, charitable registration, and the like – were all worked out with the diocese. I was and continue to be extremely appreciative and grateful for the support of the people in our diocesan offices, and for the support of many of my colleagues. It's no exaggeration to say that their support has enabled me and our new church community to get on our feet over the last few years.

Soon we were ready for the first meeting of what we had decided to call "the new St. Albans." Easter had come, the launch on Facebook went off as planned, and ten days later we'd booked the basement of the Royal Oak pub for our first meeting. I didn't know who would show up, nor how many.

I was pleasantly surprised when 18 people arrived, enough to have us pulling in additional chairs and tables for the meeting. It was, as expected, a diverse group. Most of us were strangers, so we spent time on introductions and getting to know one another. There was a young man who'd emailed to inquire about finding work at St. Albans. There was the Lutheran who was there as a visible expression of the full communion between the Anglican Church of Canada and the Evangelical Lutheran Church in Canada. There were supporters of Centre 454 who knew we needed help to build the new congregation. There was a former member of the old St. Albans who was now well-ensconced in another parish, but who was willing to lend a hand. There was another member of the old St. Albans who wanted to return the parish to the glory days of the 1980s and early '90s. There was an advocate for the LGBTQ community. There were a handful of Anglicans who lived in the neighbourhood and were curious. There was a youth worker from a neighbouring parish. There were young adults who were looking for a different sort of church home. It was a good beginning.

You could tell right away that there was energy in the room. "This is a unique opportunity," I said, by way of moving into a conversation. "We, as the Anglican Church of Canada, haven't started a new congregation in downtown Ottawa for at least a generation. This is exciting, and it's an opportunity to do something new. But I don't want you to tell me what sort of church you want. For too long, our usual way of doing things is to have a certain form and type of church, and then to let the shape of church determine what sort of mission and ministry we do. I'd like to suggest that we flip things around. Let's start by trying to figure out what sort of mission and ministry God is calling us to in this time and place, and then we'll let that shape the kind of church that we're called to be." It wasn't a new idea, of course. Many writers have recommended that rather than have our ecclesiology shape our missiology we should instead let our mission shape our church. But we were uniquely placed to actually do it, because as of yet our church had no shape. And so the conversation ensued about ministry and mission, about the demographics of our urban neighbourhood and about the cultural context in which we find ourselves as Christians in the 21st century. We talked about Centre 454, and shelters, and the diversity of urban populations. We talked about young adults trying to find a church home and students at the University of Ottawa away from home. We talked about immigrants and First Nations people, about new Christians and jaded Christians. We talked about inclusivity and social justice. We talked about ourselves, about the ministry that we needed, and about the mission that we were passionate about. It was a healthy, holy, and energized conversation.

We continued to meet on a weekly basis. We pulled out census data to verify our anecdotal impressions, and we crunched the numbers. It turned out that in our census tracts, the proportion of young adults in their 20s and 30s was double the city-wide average. Students, singles, and shelter-residents were disproportionately represented in our neighbourhood. As a result, a consensus emerged that we should focus our mission and ministry on three specific demographics: college and university students, with emphasis on the University of Ottawa; young adults living in the neighbourhood and beyond; and those experiencing homelessness and dealing with poverty. We talked about our vision of being a Spirit-led, Christ-centred, contemporary urban church.

Discussion gravitated almost immediately to the word "contemporary." To some, contemporary meant the worship style that was developed by evangelical churches in the 1980s and '90s, with the soft-rock praise band, fancy lighting, and hip preacher. To others, it meant that we would be an intentionally diverse community, embracing LGBTQ people and other marginalized groups. To still others, it meant engaging with the postmodern sensibilities of students and young adults. And to yet others, it signalled progressive theology and an emphasis on social justice. For me, the word "contemporary" suggests that we need to explore new models of church, and to be fully engaged with contemporary culture and contemporary ways of thinking. It certainly doesn't mean trying to re-create the church of the boom days of the 1960s, nor the "contemporary" church of the 1990s. There wasn't much to be gained by simply mimicking what other churches in our city were already doing well. We would need to draw on the best of those various traditions, but we were going to have to pull it all together in a way that made sense for our community, served our neighbourhood, and gave fresh voice to the good news for our time and place.

Sometimes people ask me what I mean when I talk about letting mission and ministry shape the church. I tell them that at St. Albans, it means that there's a lot of spilled coffee. When we decided to focus our ministry on students and young adults, we quickly realized that students like to drink coffee in the morning. No great revelation there. But they also expect to be able to take their coffee pretty much everywhere they go – to lectures, work, the university library, friend's homes, stores, and, as it turns out, to church. So as a church with a ministry to young adults, we became a church where people can bring their coffee.

I remember one Sunday morning, one of our young adults sat near the front with her cup of coffee placed near her feet on the floor. As I'm starting with the opening prayers, there's a flurry of activity to my right. Someone knocks the cup over, coffee streams across our 145-year-old pine floors, which, fortunately, are more or less coffee-coloured, and several people rush back to the kitchenette to get paper towels to mop everything up. The person whose coffee spilled returns to her seat with a steaming new cup. Next set of prayers, the coffee spills again and the whole sideshow repeats itself. There's a lot of coffee spilled at St. Albans; it feels like home, and the young adults keep on coming.

FIVE

Shaping Space

Not one of the books and manuals that I managed to find on church planting suggested that the first step in starting a new congregation is to acquire a big old church building and launch a major construction project. But the first call I received when I returned home from our school-building trip in Nicaragua was from the diocese asking me to prepare a preliminary list of requirements for the St. Albans renovation project. I decided that I'd better go and take a look inside.

"Oh my God ...!"

I didn't know whether they were a prayer or just the first words that slipped out of my mouth when I walked into the St. Albans Church building for the first time. I had seen the building from the outside, but never before had I actually stepped inside. After weeks of actively thinking about how to be a "contemporary urban church," it was a bit of a shock to cross the threshold and take that initial look at our new home.

St. Albans is the oldest surviving church building in downtown Ottawa. It was built in the neo-Gothic style of the 19th century – long, dark, and narrow. If I was to stand behind the altar at one end, there was no way I could throw a football and hit the back of the church, and that wasn't from lack of height. This was a beautiful and historic space – but how were we going to be a contemporary urban church in this building?

Because space matters. It gives a feel to the liturgy, helping to shape it as formal or informal, solemn or exuberant, contemplative or noisy. It puts constraints on seating arrangements and on lines of sight and sound. It affects how we move as a community, how we transition from our initial welcoming and gathering to our actual worship and then into the coffee hour or whatever else follows the liturgy. And that's just on Sundays. Does the physical layout create separation between mid-week use and worship? Are we a church 24/7 or just on Sundays? Is our space set up to be of service to the neighbourhood? Will our physical arrangement augment or decrease the comfort level of those who cross its threshold?

Most church plants start in someone's home, or lease space on a temporary basis when they want to start having public liturgies. But we weren't just a plant. Although we would have to form a new congregation, we were also tasked with the renewal of a parish that dates back to 1865. With the parish comes the building.

That brought with it certain advantages. The church building of St. Alban the Martyr is a visible presence in downtown Ottawa, located on a main thoroughfare, in a diverse, high-energy neighbourhood. The parish had a history of reaching out to the poor and vulnerable of our city and of standing up for social justice, a history that we were thrilled and honoured to inherit. It had a geography and a neighbourhood that provided the context for our ministry and would eventually translate into our focus on students, young adults, and those dealing with poverty and homelessness. It also had an architecture that was significant, designed by the same architect who was responsible for the Canadian Parliament Buildings just down the street, and worthy of heritage status.

I soon discovered that if the doors to St. Albans Church are left open, people come inside, any time of day, any day of the week. They might be tourists wanting to get a glimpse of our neo-Gothic structure, or the incredible collection of stained-glass windows, or the wooden carvings of the sanctuary. Some have heard that St. Albans was the church home of the first prime minister of Canada, Sir John A. Macdonald, and they take a moment to sit in his pew. Some visitors are our neighbours who live in homeless shelters, looking for a moment of peace and quiet that is hard to find in their daily lives. Many simply wander in and stay a while to pray.

But there are also disadvantages to being handed the keys to a 145-year-old stone building. We were just a handful of people at the time, and the maintenance and upkeep of an old building hadn't been high on our list of priorities when we envisioned the things we would have to do as a new church plant. I remember in October of our first year, as the harsh Ottawa winter approached, someone suggested that maybe we should get the furnace serviced. "That's a good idea," was the response. "Does anyone know where the furnace is?" Eventually we found the furnace – there were, after all, only so many places it could be. But that was a minor detail. The big issue was the one that soon became known as the "R-word." The renovation.

The plan, of course, was for Centre 454 to move from its leased facilities on Murray St. into the lower level of St. Albans Church. Because the lease on Murray St. was expiring, the move was a matter of considerable urgency. But in order to accommodate Centre 454, the entire basement of the church building would have to be gutted and rebuilt. This was no minor undertaking in such an old building, and there were lots of unexpected discoveries along the way. We found asbestos in the furnace room and mould at the base of the stone walls. And when eventually the earth was excavated to the base of those walls so that the masonry could be repaired, we discovered the biggest surprise of all: the whole church was built not on a foundation of bedrock, but rather on cedar planks that had been laid on top of a great pit of sand. Sandy Hill wasn't just a cute name for the neighbourhood; it was a pretty accurate description of the ground upon which the church stood. Around most of the perimeter of the church, those 145-year-old cedar planks were in amazingly good condition, still supporting the heavy stone walls of the building. But at the eastern end, where there is a bit more clay in the soil, the cedar planks were gone, leaving a two-inch vertical gap between the stone walls and the compressed earth below. When this was discovered, I remember turning to the structural engineer who was in charge of the project and asking her what was actually holding up the church. She just shrugged and shook her head as if to say "Only God knows." We filled the gap.

Of course, it wasn't just the basement of the church building that was affected by the renovations. In years gone by, this lower level had acted as the church hall and had housed facilities such as the kitchen, the washrooms, the offices, and the Sunday school. All this space was to be turned over to Centre 454, and so changes would be needed to the church proper upstairs in order to provide the congregation with the facilities it would require. That meant renovating *both* levels. That, in turn, meant that we had a wonderful opportunity to think about church space, but within a very tight timetable.

Although the renovation project was a diocesan initiative to accommodate the return of Centre 454 to St. Albans, we needed to provide the design input for everything related to the church upstairs, and to help monitor and supervise that portion of the work. It was a major undertaking. The building itself is officially designated as a heritage site, and so the diocese hired an architectural firm noted for its heritage work, one that had previously worked at St. Albans in the 1980s. Soon the emails were coming, asking for a list of functional requirements for the church renovation, proposing dates when we could meet. This created a dilemma. We were already meeting twice a week to build up our new community, creating a vision for the new St. Albans, and working hard just to be ready for our first service in July. The last thing we needed was to divert the people doing these important tasks into building design and construction meetings. In fact, it would have been disastrous to make the building the chief preoccupation of our church-planting team.

A decision was made. I would take on the responsibility for the St. Albans portion of the renovation project, working with the architects and the diocesan team, effectively shielding our emerging community from too much involvement. I'd brief them and get their input as needed, but allow them to continue to focus their energies on building up the community, its mission and ministry. It was a good fit. In my previous work, I had acted as project manager for large construction projects, airport terminal buildings as it happened, and, as an engineer, I had background knowledge that would be helpful as we worked through the St. Albans renovation. Perhaps it was coincidence, or perhaps providence, but it certainly was convenient that the pastor of the new St. Albans happened to be an engineer with some construction experience.

The project chewed up huge amounts of time, but it was also a once-in-a-lifetime opportunity for us to think about church space, and to design a space in which to be church. Before I could get to the requirements list that the architects were pushing for, I needed to do a little homework. Books and Internet searches filled my next 48 hours. I read about the history of church space and the theologies and architectural principles that were the foundations of various designs. Good background material, but what I was really searching for was the right metaphor to guide the design work. What *is* the church building? Is it a sanctuary? Is it a "third place" between home and work, similar to the concept that inspired Starbucks and others? Is it a community centre? Is it a theatre, a lecture hall, a monument, a gathering space? Are we using it to make a statement, or to facilitate an experience of God?

In our initial meetings at the Royal Oak, one of the phrases that resonated with our team was the need to provide people with a spiritual home: a spiritual home for students arriving in our city, for those living on our streets, for people who had been marginalized, for people in transition, for those of us gathered around the table at the Royal Oak. The idea of a spiritual home became the guiding principle in our thinking about the design of the church space. Words like "living room," "gathering space," and "family room" started popping up as labels on our design sketches. One of the most important things about a home is that it is a place of belonging and relationship, of welcome and hospitality. That's what we wanted for our church.

We were going to be a church restricted to one level, and so every inch of the space had to be multifunctional. That meant putting an end to the tendency of the last century or so to move pretty much every church activity, except for the actual worship, out of the church proper and into the basement or parish hall. While I understand that the use of parish halls is convenient in many ways, the unintended consequence of moving out of the church sanctuary is often to segregate the one hour spent in worship from the other 167 hours of the week. It grieves me when I see a church building that is only used on Sundays. I wanted to see our space used if not 24/7 then at least as much as possible. With Centre 454 planning to be in the basement five days a week in the summer and seven days a week in the winter, we were off to a good start. Now we had the opportunity to design the upstairs space to maximize the usage of both levels.

The architects, however, brought a different perspective to the project. St. Albans was a heritage building, a beautiful example of 19th century neo-Gothic architecture, which we had an obligation to preserve for future generations. The idea of putting washrooms and a kitchenette in the nave of the church was initially greeted with concern. The thought that we would remove pews to create a more flexible space bordered on heretical. My desire to replace the heavy wooden entrance doors with glass doors so that people could see inside was a complete non-starter. Initially, I was focused on function while the focus of the architects was on heritage aesthetics, or so it seemed to me. We clashed and I got frustrated, finally telling the architects, "We want this to be a living space, not a museum."

"Well, then, tell me what you think a living space should look like. What is it that you're hoping all these living people are going to be doing in the space?"

Good question! And so we talked about our Sunday gatherings, about our hope that we could make it easy for people to cross our threshold, and that we could provide a gathering space near the entrance where welcome and hospitality could begin. We talked about transitioning into the worship experience and about how we were looking for a configuration that was more rounded than long and narrow. We talked about how we would transition into a coffee hour after our worship, and about how we wanted to make it easy for people to stick around. We talked about mid-week meetings, about office space and administration, about yoga classes, about being multi-generational and making children feel part of our gathering, about concerts and theatre, and about how we could reconfigure the worship space into a dining area with a minimum of fuss.

A vision started to emerge. We would leave the front part of the church, the sanctuary, intact architecturally, achieving the flexibility we needed there by the reconfiguration of furnishings and the addition of sound and lighting systems. But the back third of the nave would have to be reconstructed somehow to accommodate office, meeting, and ministry space; and washrooms and a kitchenette – everything needed to be church, seven days a week, all on one level, all in the church space.

I have to admit, it was kind of fun, a throwback to my engineering days. I found some quad-ruled paper and started sketching, moving blocks of space around, wandering around the church, pacing off measurements, testing dimensions. One idea came to mind, but it seemed a little off-the-wall. What if we created free-standing glass structures in the back third of the nave to house the facilities we needed upstairs? The next day, or so it seemed, I got a call from the architect.

"What do you think about constructing some pods in the back of the church, free-standing structures with glass walls?"

We went with this idea. The glass would give the building a contemporary look, would create a wonderful space for children, and would generate some great sight lines which enhanced the original aesthetic of the church. Underneath the basement floor, we found some of the original 150-year-old floor beams, which we reclaimed to create the wooden frame for the free-standing structures – old-growth white pine that would have been harvested by Ottawa's first settlers. Using that wood created both a narrative and a visual element linking the new additions with our history and with the traditional aesthetics of the architecture. I'm sure Sir John A. would have been pleased.

* * *

It's one thing to create a design on paper. It's another to get it to "work" the way you intend. In between, was the actual construction. It was a long process, well over a year, with remedials and finishing elements that dragged out a second year. We committed ourselves to worshipping in the church every Sunday during the construction period, even in the midst of the dust and chaos. Maybe that was foolish, but we felt that we needed to maintain a level of consistency, and there is that bit that Paul wrote to the Romans about suffering producing endurance, and endurance producing strength of character. In the end, we only missed two Sundays, when we were booted out of the building for safety reasons, but on those days our United Church friends down the street came to our rescue and provided us with space to worship on short notice.

For me, the renovation project was an endless series of construction meetings, some tedious, some hotly contested. For our community, it meant spending Sundays in a construction zone, without heat some weeks, without toilets for most of the year, and dust ever present. Not the ideal conditions for building up a community and attracting new people, but amazingly enough, new people showed up just about every week. Maybe Paul was right about that character-building thing.

The end result of the renovation, despite taking longer than originally planned, was everything we had hoped for. The space is visually stunning, with the new additions enhancing rather than detracting from the aesthetics. Functionally, it works and it is used intensively. The downstairs, which was purpose-built for Centre 454, can serve up to 200 people each day – people who come for a coffee, who play cards, who meet with counsellors, and who benefit from various inreach services such health, housing, and the like. The upstairs is no longer a Sunday-only space. It is open pretty much every day, for meetings and lunches, for yoga and small groups, as a study space for students and a calming place for neighbours who want to pray or who just need a little peace and quiet. One moment it is a worship space, the next it is a community centre, shifting back and forth until the boundary between the two uses starts to blur.

Much has been written recently about the "missional" church, a church that goes out into its neighbourhood to serves its neighbours, a church that takes the gospel beyond the walls of its building and engages society. The missional church is often contrasted with the "attractional" church, the church that gathers in its own building, offers programs, and hopes that people are attracted to come. I think that the missional-church movement is a great thing. Churches *do* need to get out of their buildings and into their neighbourhoods. We try to do that, as individuals and as the St. Albans community, by spending time on the university campus and in local coffee shops, on the streets and in our local shelters and social service centres, encouraging people to live gospel lives wherever they are. But sometimes the missional versus attractional concept can be set up as a false dichotomy. One way to be a missional church is to use the church space for mission. We can bring the neighbourhood into the building by using the building to serve the neighbourhood. Our neighbourhood needed a place where people living in homeless shelters could find some peace and quiet, or even do some yoga. Our neighbourhood needed a 200-seat venue for the arts. Our neighbourhood needed a day program for the homeless. Our neighbourhood needed a space where social justice groups could hold educational events. By incorporating all these community needs into the re-design of our worship space and by encouraging a wide variety of activities to happen within our space, we become a missional church not just beyond our walls, but also within. And the boundaries that we've become so accustomed to begin to blur, for the better.

SIX

Welcome.
Explore.
Connect.
Serve.

**Did I mention that we would never have picked
July 3 as the date of our first public worship service?** Not only was
the timeline too tight, but it made no sense to build momentum towards a launch event only to see everyone disappear to their cot-
tages and vacations immediately afterwards. But sometimes you just
take what you're given and work with it.

Our initial team waxed and waned as we continued to meet
weekly through the spring of 2011. Those who were hoping for a
return to the glory days of St. Alban the Martyr left and wished us
well when we stuck to our vision of a contemporary urban church. A
few, when they realized that we would continue to draw on the liturgies and sacraments of our Anglican tradition figured that that
wasn't their cup of tea, and they left too. But others drew in, and we
kept on meeting and talking. Soon enough it was time to take stock
of the commitment level around the table. We had an idea of where
we wanted to go. Now we needed to know who was in, and who

wanted to work their butt off to get us up and running. Visioning and planning are all very good – but it was time to execute.

So in addition to our Wednesday evening meetings, we set up a working group that met on Saturday mornings to start crunching the nuts and bolts of getting a church up and running. These ten people formed the core group that would carry our community for its first year and beyond. That first Saturday morning we began with prayer, and we continued with a whiteboard. We drew a big cross in the middle and at the four points we wrote Worship, Mission & Ministry, Spiritual Growth, and Community. Then for each of those four areas, we jotted down some key words and thoughts, and started to generate a list of what needed to get done: campus ministry, small groups, communications, sound and video system, readers, prayers, pastoral care, renovations, courses, children and youth, Centre 454, and lots more. It was a long list.

Music quickly worked its way to the top of the list. It had already been the subject of many Wednesday evening conversations. We knew that singing mattered, and we were blessed on our core team with a couple of talented musicians who agreed to lead music and to start the process of selecting and teaching songs. We were a 21st-century church, so we wanted a good proportion of our music to be from the 21st century, with some of the greatest hits of previous centuries mixed in for good measure. Our musicians started sorting through a variety of sources. Songs from the radio, indie artists, recordings by other churches, classic hymns that could be reworked, a selection of contemporary Christian music – all of these yielded nuggets that could be worked into our playlist. The result was an eclectic mix, a fresh sound that gets people's attention, no more so than when the music of Metallica made its first appearance on a Sunday morning.

"The music is different here," remarked one visitor after her first Sunday at St. Albans. Not many churches incorporate U2, Coldplay, and Mumford & Sons as part of their Sunday morning playlist. Of course, those aren't the only songs we sing. We like variety – classic hymns, contemporary praise, rock, country, spirituals and folk all make an appearance during Sunday worship from time to time. It's become part of what we mean by "contemporary urban church." We value diversity and inclusivity, we channel urban energy and we push boundaries. We try to reflect that in our music. The songs we choose speak to us and allow us to participate in worship in a variety of different ways and different styles. Sometimes the lyrics speak to us in a direct way, sometimes in a highly ambivalent way – what is Dylan really talking about in "Every Grain of Sand"?

But it's about more than how the music moves us on a Sunday morning. We sing Mumford & Sons at St. Albans so that when people are listening to their playlists on a Tuesday or a Saturday, connections start to happen. Our Sundays start to shape our Wednesdays, and our Thursdays start to shape our Sundays. We invite people to pay attention to what they listen to during the week, and when the words and music move them, to send us an email or tweet saying "I heard this great song, and I think we should use it on a Sunday."

Musically, we were off to a good start, but we still had to pull together our first service. We needed a keyboard. Would we have a children's program? How do we get keys for the church? The details were enough to boggle the mind, but perhaps the most important thing was to decide how to worship in a way that would set the stage for the community we hoped to become. We had decided that July 3 would be a diocesan event; a more public, neighbourhood launch would have to wait until September when folks were back from summer holidays and university students were back in town. We knew that the bishop would be coming on July 3. Then, unexpectedly, we received a request for a baptism from a young family in the neighbourhood. Well, why not? We were there to serve our neighbourhood, so why not start right away? And the symbolism was a good fit for a parish about to be reborn.

So we pulled together a liturgy around the sacraments of Eucharist and baptism, and we chose some great songs and taught them to our Wednesday night group. We made it informal and interactive, with lots of participation, and we put the whole thing into a printed booklet so that no one had to juggle books. Sunday arrived, and folks came from all over the city to show their support and celebrate our new beginnings. We all wrote down our hopes and dreams for the new St. Albans and placed them in the offering, a gift to God, and guidance and inspiration for the leadership team. We knew that it would be a long time before we'd see that many people again on a Sunday morning.

I have to admit that I was getting a bit run down by the time we finished that first service, and there wasn't much in the tank for Sunday number two. But just as I was dragging my feet around the church getting ready to go the next Sunday morning, a big yellow school bus rolled up to the front door, and out poured my former parishioners from the Parish of Huntley. "We thought you could use a little support," one said as we exchanged hugs, and she was right. It's one thing for people to hold you in their prayers, and we appreciated all the prayer support we were getting for our new venture. But it's another thing to have people actually show up and hold you in their arms. And I think that was just what I needed at that moment.

It was healing for them, too. Some of the Huntley folk had been downright angry when the bishop announced to them that I would be leaving to go to St. Albans before I'd even finished my third year in Carp. They had every right to be upset after all the time we'd invested in building up our relationship and after all the effort they'd put into training me how to be a half-decent priest. But at least now they had a sense of what I'd been called away to do and why Bishop John had thought it important enough to cause them some disruption. And so, surrounded by people I loved, we had another joyful celebration in the new St. Albans with a full church for the second week in a row. There was the busload of Huntley people, there was our core group, and there were people from a neighbouring parish who had decided to worship with us for July. But just as importantly, given our future aspirations, there was a smattering of people who had come the first Sunday and liked it enough to show up again. Some of them brought their friends, and one of those friends even turned out to be the drummer we'd been hoping for.

Soon enough, though, the carnival atmosphere of July was over. As expected, our Sunday numbers dropped into the teens during the hot, sultry days of August. That was okay. It gave us time to get to know each other, to develop a bit of a rhythm to our worship, and to prepare for our real launch in September. It also gave us a chance to learn a little something about hospitality. Often, churches looking to grow tend to focus on getting people through their doors for the first time. More important, however, is whether those same people come back for a second and third time. Though that depends on many things – music, preaching, and the like – the most important factor for many people is whether they feel welcome.

On one of those late summer Sundays, I was coming down the aisle toward the door of the church as the last verse of the last song was being sung. A man walked in through the main entrance carrying a mattress. This puzzled me, so I went over and asked him, "Why are you bringing your mattress into the church?"

He replied, "Because that nice lady over there told me I should!"

I saw that he was pointing towards Carrol, but I was still a bit confused. A few more questions clarified things. Turns out that he was in the process of moving, and he had been walking down the street past the church with his mattress. Our singing attracted his attention, so he came in to listen. Carrol had noticed. She went to talk with him and invited him to join us for refreshments after the service. But his mattress was still outside, and there was a risk of rain. So Carrol had told him to bring in his mattress, and that's just what he was doing as I was walking down the aisle. Our guest with the mattress stayed for refreshments, and then he left, to continue with his move. But he was back the next Sunday. Hospitality means welcoming people as they are. Even if they're carrying a mattress.

I often ask people why they come to St. Albans, why they decided to join our community. One of the answers I get most often is that they decided to join because the *second* time they came on a Sunday morning, someone greeted them by name. It may seem like a small thing, but it matters, and it takes an intentional effort by people in our community to *make* it happen. On Sunday mornings after the service, during coffee time, a quick look around the church will often reveal a number of people scribbling down names or typing them into their smart phones.

We do sometimes experience a tension when it comes to welcoming. We want to be an all-ages church rooted in our neighbourhood, but we have a ministry focus on students, young adults, and those who are homeless. As a result, there have been occasions when older people have wondered whether they are welcome. At times, their wondering has been triggered by careless remarks made by some of our younger people, who have a hard time containing their enthusiasm about the youthful composition of our community. But it has often been the older members of the community who have taught the rest of us about hospitality, remembering names, accepting the ministry focus on a younger demographic with grace, embracing a worship style that takes them out of their comfort zone, welcoming newcomers and visitors of all ages, and, on the odd occasion, encouraging someone to bring his mattress into the church.

It shouldn't have been any surprise then when "welcome" emerged as one of our core values at our first fall retreat. The retreat was a chance for our community to relax and recharge after the busyness of our September launch and the start of campus ministry at the university. It was an occasion to get to know each other better. But it was also an opportunity to reflect on the core values of the church, which were starting to emerge, and to articulate them in a way that would guide us going forward. First, we talked about our "sparks," the things we were passionate about and that generated energy for us both as individuals and as community. Then we tried to take those sparks and that energy and translate them into core values, action-oriented statements that we felt the Spirit was calling us to embody as a community. There were good conversations, and there were disagreements.

In the end, four core values *did* emerge, which in their simplest form could each be reduced to a single word: welcome, explore, connect, and serve. These were the verbs that would lead us forward, the touchstones that we would come back to time and time again. We were learning how to be a welcoming community. In time, we would deal intentionally with "connect" and "serve." But what would it mean to be an exploring community, a church that values exploration? We imagined that it might mean trying new things, allowing ourselves to experiment and to do things differently than they'd been done in other times and places. We imagined that it might mean creating a culture where people felt free to ask questions, knowing that the answers aren't predetermined. We also knew, some of us from personal experience, that in many expressions of church the sort of exploration we were envisioning was difficult or even discouraged, because of the challenge it might pose to the authority of the leadership and the tradition.

SEVEN

The Authority Thing

The musicians and I were hanging out, talking about songs and a couple of set pieces of liturgical music that we could do as part of our Sunday worship. It was a good conversation, with plenty of creativity and enthusiasm. Social media and the Internet make it easy to generate song ideas and to sample music these days. Many new churches put their music online or on YouTube to make it accessible. Still, it occurred to me that since we were going to be following the liturgical calendar, it might be useful to have a hymn book as an additional resource for those Sundays when we would be trying to highlight church seasons such as Advent or Lent. So I suggested to our musicians that we might want to have a look at *Common Praise*, the hymn book produced in the 1990s, which was in common usage in the Anglican Church of Canada. I was taken aback by the response.

"To be honest, much of what's in that book is not music that I find worshipful," replied one of our musicians.

We'd been mindful to that point of trying to build a playlist for St. Albans that would speak to our experience and help us articulate the emerging voice of our community. It was important to us that the musicians were able to lead songs that they connected with in order to be as authentic as possible.

And so the book was set aside. We still had five months of what church people sometimes call "Ordinary Time" in front of us, so it would be a while before we really had to worry about the special seasons of the church year. Better not to stifle the creativity that was emerging in our music.

A couple of weeks later, those same musicians sent me the list of songs that they had carefully and prayerfully selected for our first worship service in July. I was surprised to see that two out of the four songs could be found in the pages of *Common Praise*.

Two months later, I experienced something similar. Our practice was to have a rotation of volunteers write and lead the prayers that we use in the middle of our service. People were doing some good creative stuff, riffing on various poems or songs. One Sunday, however, there was no volunteer. When we arrived at that particular place in the service, I asked people to pick up the green prayer books, which were available, and announced a page number. We used the prayers that were written there. After the service I got all sorts of flak.

"We don't want to use the prayers from the prayer book."

"We're going to have to do a better job of making sure that someone from the community is writing the prayers."

You get the idea. And in principle, I agreed.

But in a small community, once in a while things are going to slip through the cracks. A few weeks later, we again had a hole in our volunteer schedule and there was no one to do the prayers. This time, though, I tried something different. Instead of asking people to pick up the prayer book on Sunday, I copied some prayers out of the online version of that same book ahead of time and pasted them into the printed booklet that we produce each week. When the time came, we prayed them together. Same prayers, from the same book – but this time, not a whisper of concern.

What's going on?

It slowly dawned on me that at least part of the answer is "the authority thing." These books – the hymn book, the prayer book –

represent authority, someone else's authority, someone else's authority being imposed on us. That is what the books are after all; they are authorized texts. But our printed booklet, that's something we generate for ourselves, week after week. It's *our* voice. It's authentic. It's a genuine expression of the community. We're well aware that it's not all original material, but we are the ones borrowing what we want and putting it together with our original stuff.

This shift from authority to authenticity is what Charles Taylor identified as the defining feature of the massive social change that happened in the second half of the 20th century, and it was playing out before my eyes in the battle between book and booklet.

In her book *The Great Emergence*, author Phyllis Tickle identifies the issue of authority as the key question that the church has to negotiate whenever it enters a time of massive change and reconfiguration. She likes to characterize these periods as "great rummage sales," which happen roughly every 500 years, and she thinks that we're in the middle of one right now. As Charles Taylor puts it, "For many people today, to set aside their own path in order to conform to some external authority just doesn't seem comprehensible as a form of spiritual life."

We see this playing out in the oft-cited statistics about the "spiritual but not religious." In 1999, 54% of Americans characterized themselves as religious, but not spiritual. Ten years later, in 2009, that number had dropped to just 9%. Why such a sudden change? To a great extent, it's because of the association of religion with authority, and spirituality with authenticity. As with most social changes, there are generational factors at play. There are risks in making generalizations about entire demographic groups; but, at least in my experience, questions of authority and authenticity are front and centre for young adults in church in a way that they aren't for older people.

I have seen this play out with my own eyes in my life as a parish priest. In my first parish, we had an older demographic. I was one of the younger adults. When we gathered around the parish council table, for example, there was a basic assumption, unstated but clear: when there is a problem, the priest should be part of the solution. Whenever there was a problem to solve or a decision to be made, most people in the parish automatically assumed that, as the priest, I would have something useful and constructive to say or do about it.

However, as the new community of St. Albans began to take shape, principally as a community of young adults, the dynamic shifted noticeably in the opposite direction. The unspoken, perhaps unconscious assumption around our parish council table was that the priest might be part of the problem. This wasn't malicious, nor was it directed at me in particular. It was just an underlying assumption on the part of a number of our young adults. They had a different understanding of and relationship to church authority than did the older parishioners in a more traditional parish like Huntley. The priest was both the symbol and the representative of an externally imposed authority, and therefore was to be regarded with caution.

One day, I suggested to our St. Albans parish council that we might want to consider hiring someone for a few hours a week to do the printing, copying, and folding of our weekly booklet, something I was doing at the time.

Someone asked, "If we *do* hire someone, what would you do with the hours that are freed up?"

Good question. I answered that I thought it would make sense for me to spend more time on the university campus, developing our ministry to students. In response, another person chimed in that maybe then, instead of hiring someone to do the booklets, we should be hiring someone to do campus ministry, and that the priest should continue doing the printing and copying!

Another time, one of our leaders was starting a small group in his home, an important part of our ministry and a great way to build community. When the first session was scheduled, I mentioned to him that I'd like to come to the meeting. He hesitated. There was a look of concern.

"Why do you want to come?"

"I thought it might be helpful if I showed some support for what you're doing."

He invited me to come along, but the concern remained. When I asked him about it later, he told me that he and others were trying to create a group free from people having to speak or be in a particular way because an authority was there. The vision was to create a space where people could communally explore God without having an authority figure to turn to for the "right" answer. The vision was a good one and the group has endured as a space for people to ask questions, to struggle and to authentically engage their faith. I'm always welcome, and I do drop in once in a while – but not too often.

All in all, I think that this move from authority to authenticity is a good thing. It encourages people to think for themselves and to take seriously their own experience of faith. It creates engagement and participation in the life of the church. For many of us, including me, it takes some adjustment. But regardless of the adjustments involved, regardless even of whether one thinks this shift is a good thing or not, this is our new reality and the church needs to understand it and lean into it. That shouldn't be so hard. After all, Jesus is a prime example of one who questioned the prevailing authorities of his day, and so he should serve us well as a role model for our own time.

It's also important to say here that the young adults I encounter are *not* opposed to governance. They're not anarchists, and they have a healthy understanding of the need for any organization, including a church, to have leadership and a good governance structure. In fact, our community is generally quite accepting of the usual governance structure of a parish in our diocese, with its various rules and governing bodies of council, corporation, and vestry. What is really at stake is the way in which we as a community negotiate the questions of belief, action, and control. Who or what becomes the arbiter when there is a disagreement?

It is, as Phyllis Tickle reminds us, a question with a history. In Western Christianity, the answer for centuries was that authority resided in the hierarchy of the Catholic Church and was based firmly on tradition reinforced by apostolic succession. In the 16th century, that authority was challenged in the Protestant Reformation. Eventually, a new source of authority was proposed: Luther's principal of *sola scriptura*, only the scriptures and the scriptures alone.

The authority of the Bible has been the dominant influence in Protestant Christianity since Luther, but that dominance has also been challenged. Biblical criticism and liberal theology began to enter public consciousness in the second half of the 19th century. In tandem with Darwin's evolutionary theories, these began to chip away at the authority of the Bible as it had been generally understood. Defenders of the inerrancy of scripture emerged to counter this "liberal" influence. The term "Fundamentalist" entered the Christian vocabulary when a statement of five principles or fundamentals was issued by the Conference of Conservative Protestants in 1895. The battle among Protestants over biblical authority and what that means had been engaged.

People who come to St. Albans, both young and old, are awash in the downstream currents of all these battles. We know only too well the disputes over biblical interpretation and authority amongst Protestants. We are all too familiar with the prescriptions about contraception, and with the abuse scandals that have eroded the hierarchical authority of the Catholic Church in our society. And we are living in the age of authenticity, where the focus is on the individual and his or her experience rather than on allegiance to any external authority. But as a community and as individuals, we still have to wrestle with questions of how to act and what to believe, questions of ethical and theological vitality that are part of our individual and communal life. Where do we turn for guidance, if not for arbitration?

This isn't an easy question to answer, and at least part of the answer, for us, is a willingness to be a community of exploration, and a place where questions can be asked without answers being immediately imposed. But as a church community in the Anglican tradition, I think that we are well situated to work through these matters. We are part of a tradition that has never embraced a sole-source answer to the question of authority. As far back as Richard Hooker in the 16th century, Anglicanism has embraced, in matters of authority, what has since come to be called the three-legged stool: scripture, reason, and tradition. Hooker, while clearly a Reform theologian, never accepted the Reformation position of *sola scriptura*. His multi-faceted approach to discernment in matters of order and doctrine has contributed historically to the distinctiveness of Anglicanism and to its position as a *via media*, a middle way between Catholicism and Protestantism.

From our perspective today, I believe that this multi-polar approach is a gift. It is a more accurate reflection of how many of us actually approach matters of discernment, guidance, and authority in our own lives and in the church today. We like to engage in an authentic discernment process that attempts to balance, negotiate, and engage with multiple sources of wisdom and authority. We study the Bible and take it seriously, we honour and respect the wisdom of those who preceded us in the faith, and we use our brains and the knowledge we obtain from the whole variety of fields of human inquiry. In this process – in the back and forth, in the argument and counter-argument – we encounter one another, we build community, we are led by the Spirit, and God's wisdom emerges, perhaps not perfectly, but clearly enough for us to move forward without having to claim a monopoly on understanding what God intends.

However, I don't think that it is sufficient to have just three legs on the stool. For our community of St. Albans, we needed to add two more. The fourth leg on our newly constructed five-legged stool is experience. We have a vision at St. Albans of being Spirit-led, and that means, at least in part, that we believe that we can experience God. Spirituality is important to us. When author and religious historian Diana Butler Bass came to speak to us in October 2012, she defined spirituality as "an experience that connects one with a deeper sense of self and the divine, where authority is validated through internal sources." Our experiences matter to us and they inform our faith – that's how we understand things in this age of authenticity. And, to be fair to Hooker, he never meant to exclude experience from the stool in the first place. Hooker's 16th-century concept of reason was much broader than the post-Enlightenment concept that we are more familiar with today. For Hooker, reason encompassed not only rational thinking, but also intuition, contemplation, experience, and observation. And so experience, individual and communal, articulated, discussed and interpreted in community, is part of our discernment process, the fourth leg of our stool.

The fifth leg is closely related, and that is the community itself. As a community of faith, we are a *praying* community and a *listening* community that believes in the presence and power of the Spirit of God in our midst. Therefore in matters of discernment, we trust the "wisdom in the room," a wisdom that emerges not as a sole source of authority, but as one of the legs of the stool in our multi-polar approach.

Again, this is not a new idea, but simply one that needs to be articulated. It bears resemblance to the Catholic doctrine of reception, which holds that for a rule to be an effective guide for the believing community, it must be accepted by that community. It is also similar to the understanding of how God's Spirit works in gathered assemblies, an understanding that undergirds our respect for the synods of our current era, and for the church councils of the past. Sometimes it's messy, and sometimes it's ambiguous, and sometimes conflicts will emerge. But in spite of all this, there is a good that emerges in asserting the community as one of the legs of our stool. The community becomes an active rather than a passive player in the discernment process, and that in turn means that we're all learning to engage with our faith, and to listen for the voice of the spirit in our midst and in the voices that surround us.

To repeat the question that Tickle insists must be asked in times of transition in the church, where, then, does authority come from? Authority comes from God and is revealed *to* us and *through* us in a variety of ways. We are not content to say that that authority is *mediated by* or *resides in* any single source or institutional framework. Instead, we trust in multiple sources for guidance – a five-legged stool of scripture, reason, tradition, experience, and community – a multi-polar understanding that calls us to engage in an authentic process of discernment, prayer, and listening.

Will that result in disagreements? Certainly! But rather than viewing our disagreements as failures, we look at them as growing edges, occasions for learning and opportunities to embrace the other who is different from ourselves.

At St. Albans, we have a song that we often sing as our confession, in preparation for the sharing of the Peace, a song that has emerged for us as an authentic expression of the voice of our community. It goes, in part, like this:

Let us see and not destroy, let us listen, let us listen
Let us suspend judgment for the sake of love, for the sake of love
We need each other more than we need to agree,
Father, Son, Spirit, bless us with your love, with your grace
and peace.

EIGHT

Sleepless Nights

Many of the old-timers who speak to me about St. Albans have fond memories of the garden. Memories of a lush green space in the midst of urban concrete. Memories of a strawberry social, or a Palm Sunday procession, or a mid-summer barbecue. But I have no fond memories of the garden. For me, the garden was a nightmare. Or to be more precise, the source of recurring nightmares.

When I first arrived at St. Albans, the whole neighbourhood was one big construction zone. The condominium market in Ottawa was booming, and concrete and glass structures were chasing the sky as fast as the cranes could hoist them. One of these high-rises was being built immediately to the north of the church, and the contractor had arranged to lease a 15-foot strip of the St. Albans garden as a construction easement and storage area. On the east side of the garden, the city was doing roadwork. The sidewalk that separated the garden from the street was being replaced. As a result, the fence that secured the garden had been removed and the space had been left wide open. Open, but by no means vacant. In one corner, someone had set up a little sleeping area, complete with ladders rigged over the back fence as an emergency escape route. Depending what time of day you happened to wander through the garden, you could find drug users shooting up, or prostitutes turning a trick. There were used needles everywhere, and even a few caches of clean needles half-buried for future use. And that was during the day. I didn't dare visit after dark.

At first we thought, naively, that a simple cleanup would suffice. We got rid of the bedding and disassembled the ladder escape route. One of our people heroically volunteered to cut the grass and was greeted by the crunching sound of discarded needles as they were sliced up by the lawnmower blades. The place looked better, but nothing changed. The bedding was back the next morning, and the needles returned. That afternoon, I went into the garden to find a large, tough-looking man reclining on the newly cut grass in the sun, talking into his cell phone. When I looked his way, his eyes locked on to mine just for a second, as if he was daring me to try to kick him out. I didn't. He resumed his conversation. I left, worried that our church garden had turned into a place where deals get done, worried that one day a child would be hurt with a needle.

I was in over my head, so I turned to the professionals at Centre 454, which was still at its rented premises on Murray Street, for advice and support. I did that often during my first year at St. Albans, especially when it came to street-related issues. Together, we took action. We arranged for a local group of volunteers, the "Needle-Hunters," to do a sweep of the property and safely dispose of all the needles they found. We asked them to include our grounds on their regular route. We contacted the police and gave them permission to come onto our property 24/7 as required. And, with the help of the condo construction company next door, we put up a temporary fence to secure the garden from the street.

The first night after the fence was installed someone found a way to wiggle in-between the fence and the church wall. The next day, we secured the fence to the wall properly. The second night, someone tunnelled under the fence to get into the garden. The next day we were back at it, filling in the dug-out area, lowering the fence and securing it once more. I fully expected someone to climb the fence, or to cut a hole through it on the third night. But nothing

happened. Our nocturnal visitors moved on, and the garden was reclaimed. Not that we would use it for another 18 months with all the
construction going on. But at least I could sleep better.

During the dot-com investment boom of 1999–2000, one of the
trendy questions in the corporate world was "what keeps you up at
night?" It was a question that board members and investors liked to
ask as a way of prompting business executives to identify the key
risks and drivers of their business, and as a not-so-subtle reminder
of the total commitment that was expected of them in their roles as
corporate leaders. Whenever my investors asked me that question,
I usually found a way to name some of the key business risks going
forward; but in truth, in those days, there was rarely anything that
kept me up at night.

That changed during my first year at St. Albans. Perhaps it was
the newness of what I was doing, or the weight of expectations – my
own and those I perceived from others. Perhaps it was the fragility
of our nascent community, or the real risk of failure. Whatever it
was, I found myself lying awake on more than one night, involuntar-
ily going through my mental checklist, trying to ignore whatever
problem had captured my nocturnal thought processes. We knew
we were fragile in the fall of 2011. Long days on campus in September had attracted a handful of university students. Our fall promotional campaign had caught the attention of several people from the
neighbourhood and our fall launch event was well attended. But the
core St. Albans group still numbered fewer than 20 people, and that
was before Andrew and Ericka announced that they were leaving.
Andrew and Ericka had been key players in our initial launch.
Andrew had developed much of our messaging and our communications materials, and he was an important part of the music team.
Ericka was one of our leaders, and one of the most active and committed members of our community. But her work was taking her to
Vancouver, and so they would soon find themselves on the other
side of the country. They assured us of their prayers, but no longer
of their presence.

I could sense the nervousness in our core group. With all the effort that had been put into welcoming new people to our congregation, we just weren't ready to start saying goodbye to anyone yet. It didn't help that Andrew and Ericka's last day was Thanksgiving Sunday. Our community has a disproportionate number of students and young adults, and many of them leave town to be with family on holiday weekends. The few of us who were left in Ottawa gathered at St. Albans on our first Thanksgiving Sunday to be with Andrew and Ericka one last time, to bless them, to send them on their new adventure, and to give thanks, because as the good book says, we are to give thanks in all circumstances.

No one really knew what to expect the next Sunday. Would the vitality and optimism of previous weeks still be there? Would our numbers drop even further? What would we encounter? Looking back on it, I think that what we encountered that next Sunday was the divine sense of humour. Our attendance doubled. And numbers were up even more the next Sunday, too. Now, I'm sure there were a host of reasons why so many new people joined us on those two particular Sundays in October. And it was definitely the case that our core group once more rose to the occasion, filling the gaps left by the departures. But I also like to think that it was God's way of saying to us, "Chill out guys, I've got things well in hand. I appreciate everything you're doing and all, but when it comes right down to it, this is my church, and it's not going to depend on any particular individuals coming or going."

Fall turned to winter and by then we were well into our construction project. The downstairs was being completely gutted and rebuilt to accommodate Centre 454's return. Washrooms, a kitchenette, office space, and a children's area would all have to be rebuilt upstairs in the church proper. It was a huge project, and it only grew and became more complex as problems related to the 145-year-old structure of the old stone building were unearthed.

Despite the extent of the construction, we resolved that we would continue to have Sunday services in the church each week. Little did we know what we were getting ourselves into. The week that demolition started in the basement, I walked into the church upstairs on the Friday and couldn't believe my eyes. Even though the upstairs work had yet to begin, dust from the basement demolition filled the entire vaulted structure of the church. I couldn't see the pews just 20 feet away, and who knew what sort of toxins might be contained in that more-than-a-century-old dust.

But once more the community came through. The call went out for all hands on deck the next day, to dust and vacuum and clean and sweep, and by Sunday we were ready to go once more. For the next 12 months we lived with dust. We lost our toilets for six months and had to use an outdoor porta-potty – not an easy or comfortable prospect in the depths of an Ottawa winter. We lost our heat, too, thankfully not during winter, but well into the subsequent fall season. Through it all, we worshipped in the church every Sunday but two.

We were about a third of the way through the construction schedule when I received a tap on the shoulder one Sunday morning. The amazingly talented woman who had been leading our music wanted to tell me that she was going to have to step back from the music role because she was expecting her second child. I knew that "Oh shit!" was not the proper response, so I said "Congratulations!" and I really *did* mean it. But we now had one more thing that needed sorting out, and I had another sleepless night.

There are people who say that every problem is a new opportunity. I'm not sure I believe that, but in this case the problem of having to find a new music leader was an opportunity for me to learn something about what it really means to be "Spirit-led" as a church. A few months earlier, I had received a large brown envelope in the mail. Inside was a letter from a new grad looking for a job, complete with a CV and couple of DVDs of his recorded music. He was in his final year of university in New Brunswick, a musician who had grown up in the Vineyard church, and he was looking for full-time employment as a ministry intern. I had every reason to take that envelope and drop it in the trash. At the time that the internship request arrived, we were a community of 50 people, if that, and we had no cash. Besides, having interns isn't really part of our culture in the Anglican church, apart from the unpaid theological students who do internships as part of their seminary education. And we already had one of those.

But if I have learned anything over the past few years, it is that sometimes it's good to be slow to say no. And so, I sent off a quick email to the applicant: "Hi, Zack. Thanks for your application for an internship at St. Albans. We're not in a position to do anything right now, but I'll get back to you in the new year."

That could have been the end of it, but instead, over the next few weeks, I found myself thinking about the unsolicited brown envelope. What if we were to hire someone like Zack as our lead musician and as a minister for our student and young adult ministry? Our volunteer musician's pregnancy only reinforced our need for resources to move our music program to the next level. And Zack had expressed some interest in campus ministry. Was there a way we could combine a few different things into a full-time internship position?

The idea kept coming back to me with renewed persistence over the next few months. Of course, viewed in the hard, cold light of reality, it always appeared to be a non-starter for financial reasons. But then I got a call from the diocesan office. An anonymous donor had made a large contribution to the diocesan financial campaign, and designated that half of it should go to support St. Albans. All of a sudden, for the first time since we'd started, we actually had some cash. I sent an email to our wardens, the two key members of the leadership team, and told them for the first time about the internship application and the idea of hiring someone to lead our music, and our campus and young adult ministry. They were enthused. So we prayed and emailed and Skyped, and before long we had arranged for Zack to move to Ottawa and join St. Albans as our new ministry intern.

Zack has his own version of the story. He was in the final year of his university undergraduate program and felt a call to ministry. But he was unsure about whether he should continue as a worship leader, as it was called in the Vineyard church, or whether he should branch out into other forms of ministry. He decided to try to find an internship with a church as a way of figuring out what he might want to pursue. This was no sure thing. There weren't many internships around, and of those that *did* exist many were unpaid positions. But being of an optimistic bent, and because he had grown up in the Vineyard church, Zack made a list of just about every sizable Vineyard congregation in the country and started preparing the package he would send out. It was while he was preparing his package that Zack first caught sight of St. Albans Church via a friend's Facebook post. An urban church plant in Ottawa – that was intriguing. He started following St. Albans on Facebook and Twitter, and was curious enough about what he saw to add our name to the list of the dozen Vineyard churches that he'd drawn up. It was a long shot: a Vineyard student applying to be an intern at an Anglican church that had no internship program.

In fact, the whole internship idea was a long shot, but Zack was persistent, and he prayed, and he kept hoping that something would work out. A few of the Vineyard churches wrote back. One thought they could use him as a volunteer musician. Another offered him part-time work if he could find a sponsor to support him financially. Others simply wished him well. Just when it seemed like every door was closing, he received an email from the "Facebook church."

"Hey, Zack, we've got your internship application. We'd like to talk, maybe we can make something work. Can we set up a Skype call?"

It turned out that St. Albans was serious about its ministry to university students and wanted someone who could take the lead on its campus and young-adult ministry. That was something Zack was passionate about, and by combining campus and young-adult ministry with music leadership, a full-time internship position could be created. St. Albans was even willing to pay a decent salary, enough for Zack and his new wife, Selina, to live on; enough to justify moving halfway across the country and switching, at least for now, to a new way of doing church.

When Zack and I compared notes many months later, there was no doubt in either of our minds that the whole process of how he came to St. Albans was Spirit-led. He's been a great asset to our community and to our ministry, and several years later he's still with us, no longer as an intern but as our youth and young adult minister, and as our music director. Colleagues have asked me how we ever managed to find Zack. Sometimes I give them the long version of the story. But sometimes I'll simply quote them a line from one of my favourite U2 songs: "She moves in mysterious ways."

NINE

A Church for Young Adults

Back in the spring of 2011, at one of our pub meetings, we were talking about how to welcome and serve those who are marginalized. After all, the three big homeless shelters in Ottawa were all within easy walking distance of St. Albans, and we would have a day program for those who were homeless open every day in the church basement. Ministry with those experiencing homelessness and dealing with the challenges of poverty, mental illness, and addictions was high on our list of priorities. We talked about what it was like to be marginalized in society, and we talked about how Jesus engaged with those who were marginalized in his time and place – with tax collectors and people with leprosy, and the like. It was in the midst of that discussion that one of our group, a man in his early 30s, interjected: "You know, when it comes to church, it's young adults like me who are marginalized."

He wasn't talking about social or economic marginalization. This was a young man with a good job, a wonderful family, and a home. He was, rather, speaking from his own experience of trying to engage with the church as a young adult. Many young adults are made to feel like outsiders the moment they walk through the doors of a church. They are surrounded by a sea of gray hair. The music they hear is from another age. The norms and manners of the place are those of another generation. And if, heaven forbid, they persist in remaining and try to get involved in leadership or to make some changes, they often hear those dreaded words, "But that's the way we've always done it!"

We are, at least in my tradition of the Anglican Church of Canada, an institution that has been largely shaped by the post-war boom times of the 1950s and '60s and is still populated to a great extent by people who came of age in those decades. Wonderful people it must be said, and rightly called the "great generation." But for others who have come of age in the 21st century, millennials as they are called by demographers, going to church has too often become a cultural commute, an experience analogous to travelling to a foreign land. That is why people like my friend feel marginalized.

The relative scarcity of millennials in many of our church communities has hardly gone unnoticed. In 2013, popular author and blogger Rachel Held Evans wrote a blog post for CNN entitled "Why millennials are leaving the church." The post clearly struck a nerve. It went viral on social media and in the mainstream press, with hundreds of thousands of Facebook shares and follow-up articles in the *Washington Post* and elsewhere.

In that post, Held Evans writes about her many conversations with American evangelical church leaders about why young adults are leaving the church. Drawing on the latest surveys and research from organizations such as the Barna Group, Held Evans points to how millennials find evangelical Christianity to be old-fashioned, indifferent to social justice, and antagonistic towards LGBTQ people. When forced to choose between their faith and their intellectual integrity, or between Christianity and science, many are making the decision to leave church.

The starting point of the discussion, that millennials are indeed leaving church, is certainly well supported by the latest surveys and research by organizations such as The Pew Forum on Religion and Public Life. And, as Held Evans also points out, this is a phenomenon that affects not just evangelical churches, but also mainline

Protestant and Roman Catholic churches, sometimes at even higher rates. A recent Barna Group survey indicates that 59% of American young adults with a Christian background report that they had, or have, "dropped out of attending church after going regularly."

In Canada, in the Anglican and other mainline Protestant churches, these trends started to play out in the 1980s and '90s, a full decade before they were noticed in mainline Protestant churches in the U.S., and two decades prior to the current exodus of millennials from American evangelical churches, to which Held Evans attests. The dubious distinction of having been some of the first churches in North America to suffer an exodus of young adults at least gives us the benefit here in Canada of having had more time to examine what's going on.

The leading Canadian surveyor of religious trends, Reginald Bibby, a sociologist at the University of Lethbridge, cautions us against making one-sided statements, whether about secularization or about millennials leaving church. Based on his surveys and re-search on Canadian data, Bibby thinks that what we're seeing is not increased secularization, but rather increased polarization: some people, including millennials, are leaving church; others are staying; and still others are joining and re-joining.

Prompted in part by my young friend's experience of church marginalization, but also by our proximity to a major university and the demographics of our neighbourhood, the launch team for St. Albans committed itself to developing our new church community as a place where millennials could feel at home. Our leadership is made up largely of young adults who are fully engaged in the shap-ing of the community as it grows and evolves. And while we strive to be a church that welcomes people of all ages, we do have a lot of millennials in our community. In fact, numerically, millennials are the largest demographic cohort, and more join us just about every week.

So when I encountered Held Evans' blog post on why millennials are *leaving* church, I thought it would be instructive to find out why *our* millennials are *coming* to church. I asked them via a series of surveys, emails, social media posts, and conversations. Some comments were given directly to me, and some were received anonymously. Rather than try to argue or analyze the larger statistical trends, I'd like to share, largely in their own words, ten reasons why millennials are coming to church, and to St. Albans in particular.

It's all about relationship. We come to church to deepen our relationship with God and to build relationships with each other, communion, and community. We want to belong to a caring, compassionate, authentic, welcoming community that includes people who are like us, and others who are *not* like us. One of our millennials put it this way: "Recently, I was compelled to consider church again. Part of this was a thirst for a sense of community." Young adults often find themselves trying to sort out many aspects of their lives, including the spiritual. This can be a wonderful but also scary process. As a result, they recognize the value of doing this as part of a caring community that honours their struggles and supports them in prayer and in practical ways.

We talk about stuff that matters. Millennials want to talk about stuff that matters: questions of identity, purpose, meaning, relationship, God. Stuff that matters in life, talked about in concrete and relevant ways. One millennial writes, "I decided to attend St. Albans not because of the modern music or digital bulletins, but because members seemed incredibly genuine in their mutual attempts to understand God and what Jesus' message means for their everyday realities." Another person put it this way: "I was drawn to St. Albans because it seemed like it was serious about being 'the church' and wouldn't be fussing over outdated 'traditions,' which in reality have nothing to do with the Body of Christ." By talking about stuff that matters, church becomes a place for meaningful conversation.

We can ask questions and explore answers to-gether. Millennials have questions. And they want to feel free to ask them without the sense that the answers are predetermined. "I guess what I was looking for was a feeling of shared curiosity and inquiry. In university, we are encouraged to rigorously question the evidence and biases behind claims, to have arguments on fundamental issues. Through book studies, service discussion periods, and one-on-one conversations with other members at St. Albans, I feel like I can exercise this curiosity without stepping on toes or being told just to have faith and be silent." At St. Albans, exploration is one of our core values.

This is a community where we grow spiritually. Millennials come because they want to experience church as a place of spiritual formation and growth. Through worship, prayer, small groups, book studies, and a variety of spiritual practices, church becomes a place where people develop and grow spiritually. "Church provides a rare place for millennials to experience serene calm and contemplation in our buzzing, social-media-infused lifestyles, in which filling every hour with photo-worthy activities is encouraged." It breaks my heart as a pastor that in an age when many people are spiritual seekers, the church is often not seen as a place of spiritual growth. At St. Albans, we want to reestablish that connection.

My LGBTQ friends are welcome here. Almost all young adults know LGBTQ folk. They are our friends and family. And we don't want them marginalized or discriminated against. That doesn't mean that we all hold to the same understanding of sexual ethics, whether gay or straight. We wrestle with how to incorporate Christian teachings on mutual love, fidelity, marriage, and sexuality in our lives. But as we often sing together on a Sunday morning, "We need each other more than we need to agree." And, we need to provide people from all backgrounds with a safe place to land and to stay a while as they work through various challenges – including differing views of sexual ethics, identity, and orientation – as part of their spiritual journey. All people, LGBTQ folk included, are welcome at St. Albans Church and are encouraged to participate fully in the life and leadership of our community.

Social justice is part of our DNA. Millennials want to belong to a community that is passionate about social justice, and where they can connect with service opportunities in their neighbourhood. "Why do I come to church? Centre 454 is what tipped the balance for me." If there's one message that Jesus seemed pretty insistent that his disciples get, it is that we are to care for the oppressed and the marginalized. That means we feed the hungry and provide shelter for those who need it, we advocate for structural changes to unjust systems that oppress the poor, and we welcome into our community as full participants those who are marginalized.

We get to participate and contribute. Millennials don't want to just sit there. They want to be involved, they want to participate and to contribute and help shape things. "Why do I come to church? Because of the sense that everyone is welcome to share their opinions and ideas. People are encouraged to participate in everything that goes on at the church." Recently at St. Albans, we introduced an "open space" following the sermon to allow time for discussion and reflection. When asked for feedback, here's what one millennial said: "I think it is great. My generation doesn't want to just have to listen to an authoritarian figure at the front of the hall. We want an opportunity to dialogue and question and think for ourselves."

This community engages my culture. For too many millennials, coming to church can be a "cultural commute." Many millennials find it easier to engage with a church that engages their culture. Does that mean social media, relaxed and informal worship, and a playlist that includes 21st-century music? Yes. But most of all it means that young adults themselves become the key players in creating our church culture. Instead of the old ethos "this is how we've always done it," the new normal is "let's try this and see how it works."

I feel welcome here. Not very many people will join a community if they don't feel welcome. Millennials are no different. They come to churches where they feel welcome. "The first thing that convinced me that this was where I wanted my church home to be was that everyone was so welcoming. I left after my first Sunday knowing about five people's names and when I came back the next Sunday they all remembered me. It remained easy to meet people in this community, and this made me feel at home at St. Albans very quickly."

This is a Christ-centred church. "Ultimately, the best and most important thing about St. Albans for me is that it is a Christ-centred church. It is a church that remembers what the point of everything is. I saw this reflected in every aspect of church life." Many writers and bloggers have commented on the acute BS meters that millennials have developed. Authenticity matters. A church that has forgotten who it is *isn't* a church for millennials. We are a Christ-centred community – that's why we exist. That's why millennials come.

I feel like I've come full circle. When I was a young adult, away from home for the first time at university, I was welcomed into a wonderful church community – St. James Anglican Church in Kingston – right on the corner of the Queen's University campus. It was as a part of that community that I first engaged with my faith as an adult. It was there that I made my most meaningful relationships, that I had the opportunity to talk about stuff that mattered to me, and where I experienced spiritual growth together with so many others of my age and stage of life. I look back on those years as the most formative of my life, and surely four of the best years as well. Now, it's time for me to give back, or perhaps better, to pay it forward.

One of the reasons that I'm passionate about providing a spiritual home and community for post-secondary students and young adults is because the people of St. James Kingston provided one for me when I needed it. When Bishop John first called me about St. Albans, the thing that excited me most was that the church was three blocks away from the University of Ottawa and its 40,000 students. Serving those students and providing them with a spiritual home is an opportunity for me to say "thank you."

TEN

New Media, Old Media

"We've got to keep posting. It's working!"

I remember the excitement at one of our first parish council meetings. We were a bit nervous by the end of that first summer. After the rush of July, when the curious and the supportive from around our diocese had come to visit in great numbers, we were down to a core group of about 20 people by the end of August. Not disastrous by any means, but we were anxious to see more people connect with our nascent community. For those connections to have any chance of happening, people had to hear about us first. That meant communications.

Communications is one of the central tasks of the church. After all, our *raison d'être* is to proclaim the good news. One of the best of the early church's communicators, Paul, put it quite simply: "How are they to hear without someone to proclaim him?" We need to communicate, and because this is a central task of the church, you would expect the church to be an early and enthusiastic adopter of new communications methods and technologies. Historically, that has been the case. When the commercial and military system of the Roman Empire created a network of roads that enabled mail delivery, the early church wrote letters. When that Empire crumbled, it was the monasteries that became the new centres of communication, teaching the skills of rhetoric and grammar, generating new writings, and preserving and copying ancient Christian manuscripts for distribution. When the printing press was invented, Christians were all over it, writing pamphlets, printing Bibles, and bringing the good news in written form to the masses.

So what's up with digital technologies? For some reason, we haven't been as eager to embrace the new digital technologies that have exploded since the introduction of the Internet to the public in the late 1980s. Perhaps our demographics are working against us. Perhaps the nature of the new technologies is at odds with our authority structures. Maybe it's the learning curve. Maybe it just takes time. But whatever the reason, it is time to embrace digital communications technology. As Pope Benedict XVI said in 2013, "Unless the Good News is made known in the digital age, it may be absent in the experience of many people."

When we decided that ministry to students and young adults would be a priority for St. Albans, it only made sense that social media would become the leading edge of our communications strategy. As an infrequent user, I didn't know too much about social media at the time, but I did know one thing: every day without fail, when my teenage children got home from school, the first thing that they did was check Facebook to find out what was happening in their world. If that's where they were, that's where St. Albans needed to be. So I started to play with social media, and with Facebook in particular. It was easy to use and, I have to admit, kind of fun. We would still need a website for St. Albans, that was a given, that's where people go to get the details. But social media costs less than websites, we could get them up and running quickly, and they are easy to keep fresh and up to date.

We wanted to connect with young adults, and for the 18- to 34-year-old demographic in Canada, almost all of them, over nine million, were active users of Facebook. (In the USA, by January 2015, the total number of Facebook users aged 18 to 34 was 58 million.) Most of these users check in on a daily basis, so if we could get our posts into their news feed, they would see and have the opportunity to interact with us every day. Not only was this a great way to get the word out about St. Albans, but it also creates a subtle shift in the nature of the church community. Church becomes something that happens seven days a week, not just on Sundays.

Sometimes I meet with resistance from colleagues regarding the use of social media. "Face to face is the only real way to communicate," some will say. We can all agree on the importance of face-to-face communications. But imagine if someone in the early church had said to Paul, "Stop wasting your time writing those letters, you should be communicating face to face." Or imagine if someone in the early 16th century had said to Martin Luther, "Martin, I don't know why you're bothering to write down those 95 Theses. And that plan of yours to nail them to the church door is ridiculous. People won't listen to you unless you talk to them face to face."

Communications is a "both-and" proposition. If we want to reach as many people as possible, we need to use all the channels available to us, and use them well, adapting our message content and delivery to suit the medium. Two and a half months before our first public worship service, we launched St. Albans on Facebook.

But even before that we had a communications decision to make: what were we going to call our new church community? Church plants often have funky new names like "The Bridge," "Cornerstone," "The Crossing,'" and the like – names that break with tradition and convey something of the newness and the vision of the community. Is that what we wanted? The church building we were moving into already had a name; it was named after St. Alban the Martyr and, as far as the diocese was concerned, our new congregation would simply be the newest incarnation of the parish of St. Alban the Martyr, founded in 1865 as the second parish of the Diocese of Ottawa. So who was this St. Alban? It turns out that he was a pretty cool dude, at least by third-century standards.

Alban was a soldier in the Roman legion in the Roman province of Britannia, stationed in the town of Verulamium, north of London in the third century AD. He is known to us as a man who gave shelter to a Christian priest fleeing persecution, at obvious risk to himself. Alban, observing the fugitive's prayers, questioned him about his faith, and eventually Alban converted to Christianity. When reports that the priest was hiding with Alban reached the authorities, soldiers were sent to seize the priest. Alban met them at the doorway wearing the fugitive's cloak and presented himself to the soldiers as the person they were seeking. When he was brought before the military governor and the deception was discovered, Alban maintained his Christian faith and refused to offer the sacrifices required by Roman law. He was condemned to death and beheaded that same day, becoming the first Christian martyr in England.

The story of St. Alban resonated with our visioning group. It fit with our focus on social justice, and especially with the mission of Centre 454. Centre 454 would be using the basement of the church to provide a day program, a sanctuary for those who were experiencing homelessness or who were at risk of homelessness, just as St. Alban had provided sanctuary for the fugitive of his own day. The use of St. Alban's name would be a constant reminder of the importance of welcoming strangers into our midst. It would also allow us to put less emphasis on our Anglican denomination in our communications: those who were long-time Anglicans might recognize us as an Anglican church simply by virtue of being named after St. Alban, and those who were of other traditions would not be put off by a heavy emphasis on denominational branding.

One problem remained, however. In those early days, the name St. Alban's was still closely associated with the congregation that had decided to leave the Anglican Diocese of Ottawa in response to the diocesan approval of same-sex blessings. Though by agreement that congregation would have to change its name in July 2011, there was still the potential for confusion, a confusion that would work against us in building a new congregation with a new identity. We didn't have much as we met in the pub in the spring of 2011, but one thing we *did* have going for us was that we were new, and we didn't want to dilute that distinction by being confused with an old congregation, particularly one with which we were quite different theologically. The solution to our dilemma was as simple as it was elegant. We would be the "new St. Albans," at least for the first year or so of our existence – a new congregation in one of Ottawa's most historic parishes.

I wondered at the time whether describing ourselves as the "new" St. Albans would be sufficient to communicate our new identity, or whether it would prove too subtle to provide enough differentiation. The question was answered for me in August 2011 at our first public event: the Ottawa Pride Parade. I'm not a marcher. I've only rarely been involved in public protests or demonstrations, not because I'm opposed to them but because it's just not my thing. So you can imagine my surprise when I realized that our first public event following the launch of St. Albans would be the Pride Parade. It was a matter of timing more than symbolism, but the symbolism mattered too. The parade was in August and several members of the St. Albans community organized a spot for us, and invited me to join them. I did, and it was a blast. We marched with a group of churches and the atmosphere was festive. We were surely one of the least entertaining of the parade contingents, but people cheered us anyways, not because of anything we did, but simply because we were there.

We carried a large St. Albans banner as we walked. At one point, someone noticed the banner and looked quizzical. He walked along with us for a while, looking at us, looking at the banner, shaking his head and looking puzzled. Then all of a sudden, the light bulb went on.

"Oh, you must be the *new* St. Albans!" And a big smile broke out across his face. He got the message.

As I mentioned in a previous chapter, we launched the new St. Albans on Facebook at the crack of dawn on Easter morning 2011,

playing on the Easter themes of new life and resurrection. We raced
to put together a "Welcome to the new St. Albans" video, which was
our first Facebook post. And we kept posting, using Facebook, Twitter, and YouTube, backed up by our website, to get the word out
about our new church plant.

As with any communications, the medium is part of the message. Social media is interactive and non-hierarchical, and it is dominated by a younger demographic. By its very nature it challenges
older paradigms of authority and control. We had a team of eight
people all posting as "the new St. Albans." As a group, we had a
shared vision of where we were going, but each person brought his
or her own voice and experience to our posts.

It worked. By the fall of 2011, we had people seeking us out because they had heard about us on social media and had then done
their homework by visiting our website. It's impossible to overesti-
mate the importance of a good website. In my experience, of the
hundreds of people who have connected with St. Albans and become
part of the community over the past few years, the overwhelming
majority spent a significant amount of time checking out our website
to get a sense of who we were, before checking us out in person.
That's not surprising; it's simply the way people do things in the
21st century. New people started showing up to our morning worship every Sunday. Many of them had been following us on Facebook
or Twitter for a number of weeks before they showed up in person.
What *is* surprising is that a website is still a low priority for an aw-
ful lot of churches.

New media is an integral part of our communications strategy,
but so is "old media." Few things can match the reach and credibil-
ity of newspaper, radio, and TV. I often encounter a curious atti-
tude in church circles about not wanting any press. Sometimes it's
the result of a skepticism concerning the ability of journalists to
understand church issues; sometimes it's as a result of having been
burned before. But whatever the reason, there is often a deep reluc-
tance to engage with journalists and to help them do stories on the

church. However, there is no better way to get the word out about what the church is doing, and to get a gospel word out on the issues that are important to us, than to get press coverage, and so that's something we welcome and actively encourage at St. Albans.

But you have to pick your moments. We had an early opportunity for press coverage with the new St. Albans. The "old" St. Albans, the congregation that was leaving, arranged press coverage for their last Sunday in the church building, when they held a final worship service and then marched in procession down the street to their new rented facilities. They told the story of the breakup with the Anglican Diocese of Ottawa from their own perspective. As you might expect, that angered a few of my colleagues who didn't share their point of view. Many of them urged me to "go to the press" to "set the record straight." I could have done that. But you only get so many opportunities to "go to the press." The last thing I wanted was to use up one of those precious opportunities to generate newspaper coverage that would have positioned our new congregation as some sort of combatant in inter-church warfare. No, we would wait until we could tell the story that *we* wanted to tell.

That opportunity came nine months later, in the days leading up to Easter 2012. CBC Radio's *Ottawa Morning* was looking to do a "church" story sometime around Easter, and someone put them in touch with us. The story would involve sending a reporter to St. Albans on a Sunday morning to record bits of the service and to interview members of our community. While we were arranging that visit, I decided that it would be a good time to send an email to my contact at the city newspaper, the *Ottawa Citizen.*

Hi Kelly,

We spoke last year. At the time you expressed interest in writing something on the new St. Albans, a church meeting at the Royal Oak pub, but the timing wasn't right for us. However, if you're still interested in writing something, the timing would be much better for us now. Your readers might be interested in a new church plant in the oldest Anglican church in Ottawa, launched on Facebook, began meeting in a pub, with a Twitter service ("Tweet the Pews") coming up this Sunday March 25th. Or you might be interested in the renovations we are currently in the midst of to accommodate the return of Centre 454. If you have any interest, please give me a call.

Thanks, Mark

He called. We gave him a tour of the church, which was still in the midst of our major renovation, the basement gutted and the foundations exposed. We provided him with a history of the beginnings of St. Albans in the 1860s, and told him about the beginning of the new St. Albans and about our hopes and dreams for the church. Then he left, telling us we should see something in the paper soon.

On Easter Sunday, too early in the morning, my phone rang. It was my mother. Who else would call before 7 a.m. on a Sunday morning?

"There's a picture of you in the newspaper this morning," she said. "You have to go and buy one." So I did, and I also checked the online version. There we were, right on the front page of the April 8, 2012 *Ottawa Citizen*: "St. Alban's Reborn. An Easter Sunday service tells of two kinds of resurrection." It was a good article, deftly moving from the parish's origins in the 1860s to the new community and the new vision that was taking shape:

How is this version different? Well, church leaders met weekly at the Royal Oak pub for months before re-launching. They had a Twitter service on March 25th, they have an active Facebook page, and in darkly reverent surroundings they play Metallica in homage to God. Oh, and this summer they are welcoming Centre 454 back into the basement, taking on the huge responsibility of housing a cornerstone social program that caters to the city's poor and street-battered.

The impact was immediate. Even though the paper only hit the streets that morning, by 10 a.m. we had dozens of new people walking through our doors to celebrate Easter with us.

A month later, the CBC radio piece aired on its *Ottawa Morning* show. It too was a great piece, telling the "story of St. Albans rebirth" and of its intention to "create a contemporary urban church, and then to get the word out on social media." We were able to tell our story in our own words and about a half dozen people were interviewed and spoke about why they were part of the new St. Albans. It was a great way to give people who had never heard of us an immediate sense of what we were all about.

Our communications strategy continues to use a combination of old media, new media, and face-to-face communications. It works best when we use one platform to drive traffic to another. For example, we will take a newspaper article like the *Citizen* piece and put it in the media section of our website. Then, we create a Facebook and Twitter post that links to the newspaper article on our website. These posts drive traffic onto the website and, once there, viewers have easy access to information, such as our Sunday worship times, and that's when we see them in person. We've also noticed that most of our newspaper and radio coverage is generated by journalists who follow us on Twitter and are intrigued by one of our tweets. One Sunday evening we decided to use all U2 music at our St. Al's@5 worship service, so we called it a "U2charist" and tweeted about it. Three days later, another CBC radio journalist was there with a recorder, and this time the radio piece played not just locally, but nationally. In the weeks that followed, a number of new folk who heard that clip came to visit. Some are still with us years later.

To be sure, none of these media channels replace face-to-face conversations. Our most important communications still take place when we gather together, on Sundays and in small groups, in our worship and in homes, in our preaching and in the words and gestures we share as we build relationships together. Nothing replaces the gathering of the community. But the gathering of the community can be complemented and supplemented, extended and enhanced by a whole variety of communications methods and media. In order for the community itself to be created and to grow, connections have to be made. People need to receive whatever information they require to take that sometimes-difficult step of crossing an unfamiliar threshold and entering a new place. Sometimes that's as simple as inviting a friend, and sometimes it's as simple as putting a post on Facebook to get the ball rolling.

ELEVEN

A Venue for the Arts

Upon entering St. Albans Church for the first time, two thoughts flashed through my mind. The first, mentioned in Chapter Five, was a question: "How in the world can we be a contemporary urban church in this building?" The second, however, recognized an opportunity: "This would make an incredible venue for the arts." The interior space of the building was, and still is, absolutely gorgeous. Beautiful high ceilings; wood beams and panelling; ornate carvings and decoration; warm, rich colours; impressive stained glass; and the best acoustics that I have come across in the city. It would take some rearranging, sure. The chancel formed a natural stage, but it was hopelessly cluttered with furniture. The interior lighting was dim. The building itself was long and narrow, giving it an air of formality rather than the intimacy that would enhance concerts and theatre, or worship for that matter. It would take some work, but we were going to have to do the renovation anyway, so why not design with the arts in mind?

Worship is, after all, a form of performance art. Yes, it is participative, it is prayerful, it is sacred, it is the work of the people. But it is also performance. Our scriptures, too, are bursting with performance art. When Jesus overturns the tables of the moneychangers in the temple court, it is a dramatic enactment of God's judgment against the temple. When the prophet Hosea marries Gomer, the "wife of whoredom," his entire life becomes a performance intended to call attention to the broken relationship between God and the people of Israel. When God commands Isaiah to walk naked and barefoot for three years as a sign of the impending exile of the people to Egypt and Ethiopia, it is performance art more provocative and extreme than anything modern censors would allow. The prophets speak through the arts: poetry, proclamation, and performance. Our scriptures and our liturgical tradition are treasure houses of drama, music, and slam poetry. I believe that when people stop listening to ordinary prose, God finds new ways to communicate. The prophets knew this. When no one would listen to what they had to say, they turned to poetry, to song, to drama, to stories, to parables, to images, and to performance to get their message across.

There are parallels in our own day. When it comes to church, many people think that they've heard it all before. There is a bias against doctrine and dogma that causes some people to tune out. Ask people why they don't go to church and they'll tell you that it's old school. That they're tired of hearing the same old thing, or even worse, that it's boring. As a preacher, that strikes home; the most devastating critique that one can make about a sermon is to tell me it was boring.

Yet these same people who have tuned out the church's usual way of doing things will flock to see a good play with themes of reconciliation and redemption, or to listen to a singer explore the meaning of life or the complexities of relationship through song. Drama, storytelling, song – all of these have the ability to engage us, to fire up our imaginations, and to open us to new possibilities. So why not learn from the prophets and seek to tell our stories in new ways? It seemed to me a perfect match; we needed to communicate in fresh ways, and we had a building that with a little work would make a great venue for the arts.

The first thing we needed was a sound system. One of the sad ironies of many older churches is that though the buildings themselves have great acoustics, they are often equipped with a cheap sound system, filling that wonderful acoustic space with a tinny sound that crackles on and off. Our music team at St. Albans was having none of that. Someone arranged for a buddy who was a sound guy to come into the space and make some recommendations. The first thing he did was fall in love with the space and the acoustics. The second thing he did was to design and recommend a professional sound system for us that would cost $10,000. It was more than we expected. I took a deep breath and said "okay," but I told our team that we'd have to raise the money and that I'd have to run it past the bishop's office, since at that point it was still the diocese that was writing the cheques. "Go ahead," came the response. It was just one of many times during the whole start-up process that we were blessed with diocesan support.

Next on the list, lighting. When I first walked into St. Albans it was a pretty dim place. The size of the building overwhelmed the power of the light fixtures, and natural lighting, even on a bright day, was limited. It didn't help that a number of bulbs needed to be replaced, but because they were 40 feet in the air we would have to bring in a lift to perform that otherwise simple task. We decided to start with stage lighting to brighten up the front of the nave and the chancel. For our worship, with its new focal point at the front of the nave, and for theatre and concerts, theatrical lighting at the front of the church would be a significant enhancement. For the next few months, wherever I went, I looked at lights. In churches, in museums, in school auditoriums, in theatre halls, while everyone else was looking forward, I'd be looking upwards and backwards, swivelling my head around, figuring out how the performance area was lit, checking angles, counting fixtures, newly fascinated by how light technicians and their equipment are able to create magic on stage through the art and science of lighting.

By the time we brought a lighting expert into the church, the two of us were able to figure out what we needed. Finding the right place to mount the fixtures was tricky. They needed to be high enough so as not to blind us, but accessible with a ladder so that we didn't need to bring in a lift every time we needed to adjust something. Little did I realize at the time, but that was the easy part. The hard part was when we were told how much it would cost to run electrical power to the new lighting fixtures. Heritage building, stone walls, high ceilings, long conduit runs, building codes – all of these added up to a cost estimate that made the audio system seem like a bargain. But it was now or never. If we didn't put in the stage lighting system at the same time as the building renovation, it would cost even more later.

Our lighting expert was impressed by the building's potential as a venue for the arts. "One thing the Ottawa arts scene doesn't have enough of is good 100–200 seat mid-size venues. If you put in this system, and do things right, you'll make the money back in a few years."

Of course, he was the salesperson, so we took what he said with a grain of salt. I sat down with the church wardens. "What do you think?"

They said, "Let's go for it."

So we did, and it looks like our lighting guy was right, too. Income from rentals and events are on track to have the system paid off within five years.

With the building under renovation, our quest to establish St. Albans as a venue for the arts got off to a slow start. We did manage to work around the construction schedule to do some church events, bringing in a couple of speakers and some musicians. One of our speakers, Diana Butler Bass, was kind enough not to complain about the lack of heat when the furnace wasn't commissioned on schedule. "Every church," she remarked graciously, "should be under a permanent state of construction."

Finally though, with our renovation behind us, the washrooms functional and a working furnace, things got a little more interesting when we received a call from the Arboretum Arts Festival. It turns out that our sound expert had told his friends at Arboretum that St. Albans would be an ideal venue for their summer festival. Ottawa is a great city for summer music, and Arboretum was one of the newer festivals in town. They had a knack for combining visual art, crafts, and fine cuisine with alternative rock and folk bands, and the main venue for their summer music festival was Arts Court, just three blocks from St. Albans. So we sat down with the people from Arboretum and they told us what they wanted to do. We asked a few questions, though not enough questions as it turned out. They seemed well organized and responsible, so we booked them into St. Albans for a few dates in the summer of 2013.

I was nervous about the first event. I liked the idea of support-ing the arts community and I was comfortable with the people from Arboretum, but this was the first time we were renting our building out for a big concert. There would be a lot of people, and I was wor-ried that the old building itself might be fragile. There would be a bar, and we were relying on another party for security and to make sure everything ran smoothly. My anxiety increased when I saw the event advertising and posters. After the bands played, they were bringing in a DJ and billing this as a dance party until 2 a.m. I felt like I was being pulled out of my comfort zone. Initially, when Arbo-retum had booked the space, I had envisioned a seated concert that would finish around midnight, with the take-down and clean-up go-ing until 2 a.m. Instead, the event itself would go until 2 a.m. and clean-up would take place until the wee hours of the morning. I started to imagine all the things that could go wrong, and the com-plaints that we might get from both church-folk and the neighbour-hood if anything turned out badly.

As it turned out, nothing went wrong. The people attending the event, mostly 20-somethings, had a great time and were respectful of the church building. The organizers were terrific and ran things like clockwork. The bands, well they weren't my cup of tea, but eve-ryone who was there seemed to enjoy the music. There were, how-ever, complaints. Some neighbours didn't think that these late-night events were appropriate for the neighbourhood. They were concerned about the people the events might attract, and the possibility of drugs or alcohol on the street. For some people, this was a trigger to re-engage in the previous controversy over Centre 454. They even tried to make a link between the Arboretum event and Centre 454, claiming that we were attracting homeless people into the neighbourhood late at night, despite the fact that these were the last people who could afford to pay for the admission ticket. Some neighbours offered constructive suggestions about making sure events didn't go too late and that we should pay more attention to how events are promoted.

Many of us tend to get a bit defensive, even confrontational, when we're on the receiving end of criticism. That was my initial reaction. I certainly wasn't thrilled to have angry emails about St. Albans sent to our local city councillor, the police, and my bishop. But we had made a commitment to be the best neighbours we could be, and our neighbours weren't just the poor and those experiencing homelessness, but also local business owners and those in nice houses and condos. So we sat down and crafted a more detailed rental policy, something we should have done in the first place. Events would have to end by midnight. Seated concerts would be encouraged, but not dance parties. There would be no preferred pricing to try to draw in the late-night crowd. Guidelines for promotional materials were laid out.

Then I started calling and visiting some of our neighbours, hearing their concerns, telling them about our new guidelines, and letting them know that we wanted to support the local arts community by making the church available as a venue, but also that we wanted to do it in a way that made sense for our neighbourhood. I can't say for sure that we made everyone happy, but I took it as a pretty good sign when a few months later one of our most vocal critics offered to put up posters for our events in his condo building.

* * *

Hi, my name is Ins Choi. I am an actor, a play-wright, and a follower of Christ. Not quite sure how Open Table operates, but I sense that it's the right group for this idea that I have. In Jan 2014, my play *Kim's Convenience* will be playing at the NAC [National Arts Centre] in Ottawa for about three weeks, as part of their English theatre season. It's based on the prodigal son, set in a Korean convenience store in Toronto. It's funny and quite moving.

I have a solo show that I've just performed in Toronto at Sanctuary over Easter weekend. It's called *Subway Stations of the Cross*. It's about a homeless man who delivers a message from God through song and spoken words. So, while I'm in Ottawa, I'd like to connect with a young emergent church or group to host a performance of my solo show. The needs of my solo show are minimal. Ideally, in a tall old cathedral/church or warehouse or theatre. I'll be creating a trailer of it this week and can have a package for your viewing in a couple of weeks. More info can be found on my website.

I don't know about you, but a lot of junk shows up in my inbox. This message was far from junk, however. I took one look, then turned to Zack, who had taken on the role of managing our events and rentals. "This would be great at St. Albans."

I didn't know much about Ins Choi at the time, but I did know that *Kim's Convenience* was well on its way to becoming the hottest property in Canadian theatre. It had come out of nowhere to win the best play award at the Toronto Fringe Festival, and had launched a nationwide tour. I couldn't think of anything more amazing than having Ins Choi perform his "other" play at St. Albans while he was in Ottawa.

The message ended up in my inbox because I was one of the Facebook page administrators for The Open Table. The Open Table is a partnership of churches in the University of Ottawa area, which offers a free home-cooked meal and an opportunity for community to students once a month. St. Albans is one of the partner churches, and at one point I had volunteered to help out with the social media.

My first instinct was to contact Mr. Choi and arrange for him to come to St. Albans, but I figured that would be too presumptuous. Instead, we brought the message to an Open Table board meeting to see who might be interested. To my amazement, none of the other partner churches seemed to have any interest.

I don't get it sometimes. Here was something that looked like an amazing opportunity to spread the gospel message and to connect with a demographic that we don't see on a regular basis in our churches – and nobody was interested. Maybe my background as an entrepreneur makes me a bit different. I had Zack get hold of Mr. Choi and book the show the next day.

Not long after, another opportunity flashed across my laptop screen. I came across a group called 9th Hour Theatre Company, which billed itself as presenting "stories of faith, hope, love, life, suffering, and redemption; stories that capture imaginations, challenge and inspire hearts and minds, and that stimulate discussion and dialogue evoking consideration of faith." They were just launching a local tour of *Freud's Last Session*, an award-winning off-Broadway theatre production that dramatizes an imagined encounter between Sigmund Freud and C. S. Lewis on the eve of the Second World War. I'd heard of *Freud's Last Session*, in fact I'd read *A Question of God*, the book that had inspired the play, many years ago and I'd always thought that it would make a great book study for a church group. The wheels in my head started turning again.

"What do you think about bringing this play to St. Albans and running a book study around the same time?" I asked the question at our weekly staff meeting, one of the opportunities we have to bounce ideas off each other. General enthusiasm ensued and a plan started to come together. We got hold of Jonathan, the artistic director of 9th Hour Theatre, and asked him what it would take.

"You'll have to guarantee us a minimum to cover our costs, plus a cut of ticket sales."

At that moment, we had no idea how many tickets we could sell, or even how we would price tickets, so we had no clue as to whether we could cover the base cost. But the opportunity was too good to pass up and so we were in. We had just booked the first play at the new St. Albans.

The relationship with 9th Hour Theatre proved to be a good one. *Freud's Last Session* was a great success. We even turned a small profit! More importantly, we were able to assemble a diverse audience of St. Albans folk, atheists, theatre types, and people from other churches to hear C. S. Lewis and Sigmund Freud engage in an entertaining debate between the spiritual and the scientific materialist worldviews. Perhaps the highlight was when the two actors came out after the show for a talkback session with the audience, allowing all of us to keep the conversation going. It was exactly the sort of thing we were hoping for when we first envisioned St. Albans as a centre for the arts. Two months later, we had a repeat performance with 9th Hour Theatre. This time the play, *Jesus My Boy*, written by a stand-up comic, had a Christmas theme, that explored the Christmas story and beyond from the infrequently heard point of view of Joseph.

It's a special feeling when something you've dreamed of and worked towards comes to fruition. That moment happened for me during the first week of February in 2014. In the space of eight days, we had four sold-out shows at St. Albans. The Arboretum Festival brought in two highly acclaimed artists back to back: Leif Vollebekk, a folk style artist from Montreal; and Destroyer (a.k.a. Dan Bejar), an indie rock musician from Vancouver. Both played to rave reviews: rave reviews about the music, and rave reviews about St. Albans as a venue. The critics, the musicians, and the audience alike noticed how much the acoustics enhanced the sound, and how the church architecture and design created a great ambience.

But the highlight of that special week was Ins Choi's performance of *Subway Stations of the Cross*. I'd expected it to be good. I'd seen the performance of *Kim's Convenience* at the National Arts Centre the night before, and it lived up to expectations. But *Subway Stations* was completely different. It was a one man show of song and spoken word, inspired by Mr. Choi's encounter with a homeless man many years ago in Toronto. The performance was totally captivating, audacious in its breadth, and riveting in intensity. Choi's character walked out on stage furtively, with the haunted look and wary eyes of a man who's seen too much of the down side of life. As Choi himself says about the play, it's all about faith, but it comes at you in unexpected ways, in the ramblings of a homeless man, and in the seduction of spoken word:

Baby in a manger
Maybe a bit stranger
Maybe a baby in a manger in danger
Stranger still for this baby in a manger will be of great danger to those sitting on their hills, eating their fills,
with their Jacks and their Jills,
til they're ill in their bellies and their tills fill with bills.
Because, this baby in a manger is a changer,
he's a re-arranger,
from the comic microscopic to the cosmic telescopic,
Chronically kaleidoscopic, chronologically myopic, canonically Coptic
What the heck was my topic?

Even more remarkable than the play is the playwright himself. A couple of months before the show, as we were sorting out the various arrangements, Choi called us up with an idea. Why not stage the whole thing as a benefit for those who were homeless in Ottawa? Why not indeed! Here's a man who was coming to Ottawa for an 18-day, 17-performance run at the National Arts Centre, and he wanted to offer one of his few days off to perform *Subway Stations* as a benefit for those experiencing homelessness. The demands on his time were huge. The week that he arrived in Ottawa it was announced that a deal had been signed to adapt *Kim's Convenience* for TV and a feature film. He was spending time every day writing and working on a new play. And there were rumours that an American tour of *Kim's Convenience* was in the works. No wonder that when he arrived at St. Albans to set up for *Subway Stations of the Cross*, Choi had only one request: "Could you pray for me? I'm feeling pretty tired."

* * *

Thousands of people come to St. Albans each year for theatre, concerts, lectures, and a variety of other events. The church, with its gorgeous interior and resonant acoustics, has established itself as one of the desirable venues in Ottawa. Local bands call us up to use the church to record their CDs and film their videos.

Why does any of this matter to us as a church? It matters for at least four reasons. First, we live in an age when, for a whole host of reasons, it's a challenge for many people to open a church door and come inside. By opening up our space for the arts and inviting people in for the first time, our hope is to lower those barriers for a lot of people. Second, we believe in incarnation. For us, one aspect of incarnation is that the church and its space should be an integral part of the community, an expression of the neighbourhood, and of service to all who live here. Third, there is a kinship between faith and the arts. Theatre, visual art, and music – all these are spiritual explorations in one way or another. They explore our connectedness, our sense of beauty and wonder, and the meaning of our lives. By working with artists such as Ins Choi and 9th Hour Theatre Company, we can also proclaim a gospel message through the arts in a way that is accessible to a rich variety of people.

Finally, I believe that St. Albans Church is what the Celts would call a thin place. The faithful devotion of our ancestors to the architecture and beauty of the building, and the prayers of the church for the past century and a half, have gradually formed the space itself into a place where the veil between the human and the divine has been thinned. It never ceases to amaze me how when people enter the building, they experience something. They may call it peace, they may call it beauty, they may have an experience of awe or wonder. They may not have words for it at all. But whatever words we may or may not use, I think that in one way or another for many of us who enter the space, no matter whether it's for worship or for a concert, we have this inchoate sense that we are in the presence of God.

TWELVE

Meaningful Conversation

One of the best things about living in Ottawa is Gatineau Park, a wonderful intrusion of the rocky Canadian Shield, which extends to within a few kilometres of downtown. For me, Gatineau Park is at its best in winter, when I can put on my skis and glide through forests and hills on any of over 200 kilometres of cross-country ski trails. My wife, Guylaine, and I especially like to go at night. Moonlight and fresh snow lead us to one of the backwoods chalets, where we stop and meet friends for supper. The soft glow of candlelight awaits us inside. Over the babble of happy voices, we'll melt a cheese fondue over a hot woodstove, pull out a bottle of red wine, and sit down with friends for a magical evening.

Often, the backwoods ambience, soft lighting, and pleasant exertion of just having skied up the hillside give rise to intimate conversation, an opportunity to enter into territory rarely travelled at home. But alas, not always. I remember one particular nighttime ski and supper, when, for whatever reason, the conversation had been rather pedestrian – reviews of TV shows, and the usual patter for people my age about what the kids are up to. Guylaine was particularly frustrated as the two of us skied back to the car, and she turned to me and said, "Where can we go for meaningful conversation these days?"

I really wanted to reply, "You can go to church." But I couldn't. The church should be a place where meaningful conversations take place. But I wasn't sure that I could, in all honesty, say that it is.

Where do we create space for meaningful conversation in church? Do we depend on small groups? Will it happen during the coffee hour before or after the service? Do we rely on the Christian education programs attended by a faithful few? Or do we need to create space for conversation within the liturgy itself?

If we are going to create space for meaningful conversation as part of our church experience, preaching may have to be the catalyst. It is, after all, the one place in our worship where people have every right to expect some engagement with the question "What does this mean?" There is a reasonable hope on the part of worshippers that a sermon should serve to draw meaning out of the scriptural texts and other elements of the liturgy in a way that is comprehensible and relevant to their lives. If preaching is meaningful in this sense, it only seems reasonable that meaningful preaching should be the catalyst for meaningful conversations.

Good preachers know this. They preach in ways that are engaging, telling stories and contextualizing so as to draw a response from their listeners. But rarely is there the opportunity for that response to be put into words. By the time the listener has the chance to utter any words in response, those words are often reduced to "Good sermon, Reverend." The problem with performative preaching is that even, or perhaps especially, when it is done well, the take-away can be simply the feeling of having witnessed a good performance. Without personal engagement, the story the preacher tells on Sunday soon becomes overwhelmed by the many competing stories of our lives. The hour we spend at church on Sunday becomes disconnected from the other 167 hours of our week.

So if we need a place to have meaningful conversations, and if preaching can serve as a catalyst for those conversations, what would happen if we created space during or after the sermon for worshippers to speak and to interact, if not with the preacher, then with the people sitting around them?

We follow the lectionary, which meant that the next Sunday after our cross-country ski outing was "The Baptism of the Lord," and the gospel reading, appropriately enough, was the account of Jesus' own baptism, as told by Luke. It is an event rooted in time, taking place in the 15th year of the emperor Tiberius of Rome. It is an event rooted in space, taking place by the Jordan River, just north of the Dead Sea. It is the story of a particular human being, Jesus of Nazareth, born of Mary, 30 years old. It is the story of concrete actions, of being plunged into water. It is a story of the earth.

But it is also a story of heaven. It is the story of a divine presence, which is seen and heard. When Jesus had been baptized and was praying, the heavens were opened. And the Holy Spirit descended upon him in bodily form like a dove. And a voice came from heaven: "You are my Son, the Beloved; with you I am well pleased" (Luke 3:22).

The story of Jesus' baptism tells of one of those places where heaven and earth touch each other – thin places, as the Celts liked to call them. But there are many thin places, places and moments where we can be deeply aware of the presence of God in our ordinary, daily lives.

What would happen if I asked our community to talk about their thin places in response to this story? Would they be intimidated? Would they be able to articulate their own experiences of God? Would they have anything to say at all?

It always helps if someone goes first. So I told people about one of the thin places that I still recall most vividly. I was on the corner of Division and Princess Street in Kingston, in the fall of 1981. It was my second year at Queen's University and I was riding my bike to class, as I did pretty much every morning. On that particular morning, the light was red when I got to Princess Street, and so I stopped. And in that moment, as I sat on my bike with one foot on the ground for balance, the sun seemed to turn golden, and I had a wonderful sensation of warmth, and an overwhelming feeling that God was with me. In that moment, which may have lasted a second but seemed to last much longer, I knew, I just *knew* that all was well.

So, after a brief pause, I asked the congregation, "Where are your thin places? When *were*, when *are* the moments in your life when heaven and earth touch? Perhaps you can turn and gather in a small group with those around you and share them with each other."

There was a moment's hesitation. Some looked at me to make sure I was serious. Then, the sound of scraping chairs and rustling in pews, and soon, steadily and surely, the hum of voices starting to build. The space came alive with meaningful conversations.

We did it again two weeks later, and this time I pushed the bar a little higher. The gospel text was Luke's account of the inauguration of Jesus' public ministry, so we returned to the thin place of Jesus' baptism, and how he must have puzzled over those words during the 40 days he spent in the wilderness. We talked about how he must have drawn meaning out of his experience. How that meaning was then shaped into a sense of purpose. How that sense of purpose was articulated with the words from Isaiah, which Jesus read in the Nazareth synagogue: "The Spirit of the Lord is upon me, because he has anointed me to bring good news to the poor. He has sent me to proclaim release to the captives, and recovery of sight to the blind, to let the oppressed go free, to proclaim the year of the Lord's favour" (Luke 4:18–19).

Then I said to the congregation, "Now it's your turn. Two weeks ago, we shared with each other our experiences of thin places, those times and places where we encounter something that we may later name as God. Those experiences are like the one that Jesus had at his baptism, maybe not so dramatic, maybe not quite so clear-cut, but awesome nonetheless. I believe that we're meant to draw meaning out of our experience. The meaning may not be immediately obvious. It may take days or years of reflection and interpretation. But I believe there is meaning for us in our experiences of God."

Then, as I had two weeks prior, I did some modelling based on my own experience.

"I shared with you last time an encounter I had at the corner of Princess and Division in Kingston, way back in 1981 – an experience of God's presence and a sense that all was well. At first, I didn't think much about what it might mean. But a couple of weeks afterwards, a classmate of mine, who knew that I went to church, came up to me and asked me how I could be sure that there was a God. I guess he was asking his own questions at the time. And so I told him about my faith and about my relationship with God. And I told him about my experience at Princess and Division. And over time, over many years, I've now come to believe that God gave me that experience on Princess and Division so that I could tell people about God, as I did with my classmate, and, I suppose, as I'm doing with you right now.

"So what I'd like you to do now is to turn and form small groups as we've done before, and to go back to those thin places that you talked about two weeks ago, and this time, try to tease some meaning out of them. Tell each other about your thin places, those experiences of God, or those experiences that were special in some way, and try to draw some meaning out of them. Ask the 'Who am I?' and the 'What am I for?' questions and let's see what happens."

I was well aware that these are not easy questions, not the sort of conversations that you would readily launch into with the newcomer that just happened to sit beside you on a Sunday morning. But once more there was a buzz in the air, the rising hum of many voices, an atmosphere of energy and excitement filling our space. Most preachers are taught somewhere along the way that their job is to help make the connection between the biblical story and the story of our own lives. That Sunday I learned that sometimes the best way to make that connection is to stop talking and to give the space to the community.

And so we began as a community to explore the transition from performative to participative preaching. Participation has always been an important element of our church culture. Liturgy is meant to be the "work of the people," and during our initial visioning and planning sessions we spoke of the need to involve people and to give voice to the voiceless, to attract people from the margins into our community. We recognized that many in our community, especially the younger adults, are looking for opportunities to dialogue and to question and to think for themselves. But we also appreciated the importance of good preaching. In our first community survey about nine months after we launched St. Albans, the importance of good preaching was a major theme that came back to our planning team unprompted by the survey questions. We realized that it isn't sufficient to simply rely on an off-the-cuff conversation based on the scriptures of the day. We value the preparation, prayer, insight, and training that go into a more traditional homily. How can that best be balanced with a more participative approach?

Participative preaching can take many forms. Guest speakers, lectionary-based studies, email and social media discussions before or after the sermon, open homilies, shared homilies – any of these can serve as a way of drawing more voices into the conversation. After some experimentation, we decided to create something that we (and others) have called Open Space as part of our Sunday worship. We read scripture, we move into a homily (for which I am usually but not always the preacher), and then we move into Open Space, a time for prayer and reflection, for standing up and moving around, and, for those who wish, a time to gather in small groups with those around them to discuss a question arising out of the readings and homily. We don't try to make it a conversation for the whole congregation; doing so wouldn't allow for the intimacy and participation that we seek. It is, rather, an opportunity for people in small groups to articulate something of what they have experienced in the scriptures and homily of the day, to create the link between the stories of our faith tradition and the stories of their own lives, which makes our faith both meaningful and relevant.

One of the odd things for me about our Open Space is that I don't get to hear most of what's being said. Sometimes, I might sit down and participate in one of the conversations, but often I simply hover, listening for the buzz rather than the specific words. I'll hear snippets, and I get a pretty clear sense of how much energy is in the room, and often I'll get feedback afterwards about this or that. Sometimes, a post-homiletic conversation will result in a mid-week meeting. Very occasionally, I get such a strong sense of what I would call the movement of God's Spirit in our midst that I ask people more directly what was going on for them.

One of those occasions happened exactly a year after our first conversation about thin places. It was again the Sunday when we remember Jesus' baptism and our gospel reading reminded us once more that as Jesus was coming out of the water he heard a voice that said "This is my Son, the Beloved, with whom I am well pleased." So I talked about the God-given gift of identity, and about how identity gives rise to a sense of purpose in life, and how empowering it must be to have that affirmed. Every baptism is about identity, purpose, and empowerment. For each of us, when we were baptized, whether we heard it or not, the voice of God said to us, "You are my beloved child, deserving of love and respect, and I will use and empower you to change the world."

That's who you are. That's your identity, your God-given identity, given to you by the one who created you and who therefore knows who you were created to be. Imagine what it would mean to really know and trust that this is who you are. You don't need a Facebook profile, you don't need pictures on Instagram, you don't need a fancy job or an impressive degree, you don't need to wear makeup or put on a suit. Despite all the identities that society tries to give you, or makes you try to earn, your *true* identity is as God's beloved child, right now, just as you are. But it doesn't stop there. Because as surely as spring follows winter, God-given purpose follows God-given identity. As soon as you hear the voice, it's *go* time.

One of the challenges we have in churches is that as soon as we start talking about the theological concept of vocation, some people think we're talking about ordained ministry. But that's only one form of vocation and, to be honest, in some ways it's actually the easiest route to take and the one that requires the least imagination. Why? Because, as an ordained minister, I am given an altar to work from, a place from which I can teach and heal and nourish people with the sacraments of our church. Everyone can see my altar – it doesn't take much imagination, it is right there at the front of the church.

But for most of us, in order to respond to our calling and to live out our God-given purpose, we need to create an "altar in the world," to borrow a phrase from Barbara Brown Taylor. And that takes imagination and creativity.

And so I asked our community, "Where is your altar in the world? Where is the place in your life from which you speak a compassionate word and offer a healing hand? Where in life do you do justice and witness to the love of God?"

Then I suggested a few examples.

For the mom or dad, maybe *your* altar is the kitchen table. Maybe *that's* the place where you dispense wisdom, heal broken hearts, and nourish our next generation.

For the businessperson, maybe *your* altar in the world is your desk. Perhaps *that's* the place from which you seek justice in the management of the resources that are under your control, and strive to create a healthy work environment for your colleagues and employees.

For you lawyers, maybe *your* altar in the world is the law court itself, the place where you defend the weak and stand in solidarity with the oppressed, and free the captive from prison.

For you teachers, maybe *your* altar is the blackboard or the white board, upon which, day by day, you transform the ordinary materials of chalk and dry-erase ink into pearls of wisdom in the sacrament of learning.

For you who are homeless, perhaps your altar is the street, the place from which you can bear witness to your identity and my identity as God's beloved children, even in the midst of all the chaos and suffering of life.

Maybe there are *many* altars in your world. Perhaps your altar in the world is as portable as your own body, the place from which you have arms that hug and eyes that cry and a mouth that speaks words of comfort.

And when you are ill or in need, perhaps your altar in the world is your own bed, from where you show others what it means to receive love, and to be humble and vulnerable and faithful.

With that question, "Where is your altar in the world?" we entered into our Open Space.

It was a powerful moment. You could feel it in the air, in the excitement in the room, in the buzz of voices. There were strong reactions, confirmed to me by numerous people later on. And so afterwards, I asked why by email, in person, over the phone. Sometimes it's worth probing a bit more deeply, worth articulating our experience.

It turns out that many struggle with the idea of vocation and with the meaning and purpose of their lives. On that Sunday morning, some were encouraged and empowered by the realization that what we do matters, and that what we do is sacred, no matter where our altar is in the world. Others resonated strongly because they were at a point of transition in their lives, and because transitions bring questions of meaning and purpose to the fore, and yet they lack opportunities to talk about the meaning and purpose of their lives. Others jumped straight to the question of how you can know what God is calling you to do. Some people found the conversation difficult, because vocation is so often associated with employment, and many people are either unemployed or don't find their jobs to be meaningful.

All of these mid-week conversations and questions were gathered up and used as the basis for the homily two weeks later, when the text happened to be the beginnings of Jesus' public ministry and the call of the disciples. I had a chance to offer my thoughts by putting the readings into conversation with the life of the community, and once more we moved into our Open Space and everyone had the chance to ask their own questions and articulate their own experience. It was an on-going, meaningful, and holy conversation.

We are still exploring participative preaching – how, when, where, and why. There are no formulas or right answers, but people need to have the opportunity to engage with their faith, to have meaningful conversations, and to be active rather than passive participants in our worship. It's a work in progress.

But the next time Guylaine asks me where we can go for meaningful conversation, I have my answer ready.

THIRTEEN

Something More

"Tell me about that."

Though it happens often enough, I am usually caught by surprise when people take an interest in my story. How is it that someone trained in theoretical physics ends up as an ordained Christian minister? Why would a successful entrepreneur and CEO of a high-tech company decide to become a parish priest? Why take on a church plant? As I shared in the first chapter, I do not have a dramatic, "road to Damascus" story to tell. In truth, my path was gradual. I'm tempted to call it step by step, but even that sounds more directional than it seemed at the time. I tried stuff, and when something resonated, I kept going along the same lines. What started out as a desire for a second career eventually took shape as a sabbatical year. Finally, I had the chance to do a bunch of things that I hadn't found the time for previously. Some attempts, like piano lessons, didn't go far. But the theology course I signed up for at the local seminary – *that* resonated. And so I took a second course, and then enrolled in a degree program. One thing led to another, and eventually I was ordained as a priest in the Anglican Church of Canada. Some of my more learned colleagues would say it was a process of experiential discernment.

So now I'm a preacher, among other things. As a preacher in a church that follows the lectionary, a recommended cycle of biblical readings, I wrestle with whatever texts are thrown at me each week; usually one Old Testament, one New Testament, and one gospel reading. Sometimes I look for a common theme. Often it's hard to find. Not long after I'd started at St. Albans, the lectionary handed me three texts which, at first glance, seemed unrelated. Rereading them, however, I did manage to glimpse a common theme: each of the texts was asking the "big question" of its own time and place. There was a text from Joshua that was set just after the people of Israel had finally made it into the Promised Land: no more wars, no more wandering, no more Moses. For them, the big question was "What do we do now?" There was a text from Matthew set in an apocalyptic era, a time when life was tough and violent and people were anticipating the end of the world. For these people the big question was, "When will this be and what will be the sign?" And then there was a text from Paul's letter to the Thessalonians. The community in Thessalonica, back in the earliest days of the church, had been left with the impression that Jesus would be returning at any moment. But as time passed and nothing happened, people in their community were dying. Would those people who died miss out on Christ's return?

Those were big questions in their own time and place. They were good questions. But they're not *our* questions. And so I started to wonder: What is the big question of our time and place? No doubt responses will vary. Charles Taylor in *A Secular Age* reminds us that one of the defining characteristics of our time is that there are options. But the more people I talk to, the more I think about it, the more I would say that our big question is this: *Is there more to life than what the prevailing worldview of Western civilization in this late modern era has to offer?*

Because it seems to me that many people are looking for that something more. Of course, not everyone will formulate the question in the same way. Some will talk about the pursuit of happiness. Others will hire a life coach. Younger folk might wonder what they should do with their lives. Older folk might consider a second career. Some might pursue a legacy of some sort. But it's often about that elusive "something more." It's the meaning and purpose thing, and it has to do with making connections with something greater than oneself. I think that's why people take an interest in my story and the stories of others who go against the grain, who change direction midstream, who take the road less travelled. Stories like that have a whiff of the "something more" about them, and so we're drawn to them and want to check them out.

We live in a secular age. But as discussed previously, that doesn't mean that religious belief is inevitably going to fade away. It means, rather, that there are options. In this postmodern era, we live in a state of doubt, because no matter what it is that we believe, we know that there are other intelligent, reasonable people whose beliefs are different, and even directly contradictory. A Christian or spiritual or theistic worldview no longer happens by default. If there is a dominant or a default worldview in our culture, it is more likely to be a materialist worldview leavened with secular humanism, whose antecedents are found in the mechanical science of Newton, in the transition through Providential Deism in the 18th century, and in the writings of Feuerbach and Freud, not to mention the "new atheists" of more recent years. We have little problem believing in atoms and forces, and the chemical and electrical mechanisms of brain activity are taken for granted, if not always well understood. The materialist story of the universe is powerful. The arc of this story – from the Big Bang to the origins of life, from the Greek atomists to the separation of mind and matter by Descartes, through the physics of Newton, the electro-magnetic theory of Maxwell, the evolutionary theory of Darwin, and the psychology of Freud – is compelling, and it has opened up our understanding both of the universe and of ourselves.

But as a quantum physicist by training, I've never been a devotee of this materialist worldview, or at least of the claim some would make of its completeness. I recognize its power, even the beauty of its narrative, and I don't dispute its applicability in many domains.

But when one digs deep into the world of subatomic particles, as quantum physicists do, all sorts of weird and wonderful new phenomena emerge. If the materialist worldview can't fully do justice to the world of subatomic physics, how can we ever expect it to exhaust the subtleties of the human experience or provide a complete explanation of human consciousness, let alone the spiritual dimension of human life? It's powerful, but it's too narrow. We need something that goes beyond. We continue to look for that something more.

Sometimes people ask me about favourite hymns. I tell them that mine is U2's "I Still Haven't Found What I'm Looking For." I often get puzzled looks when I tell people that. Some will scold me for singing secular music in church, especially if the second verse is included, the one about sex and desire. But to me, it is a song about longing, a song about searching, and it captures in a powerful way the quest for the something more that is a driving force for many in our current context.

For those who are looking for something more, the church should be a natural ally, a spiritual home, or at the very least a shelter and a companion along the way. But for great numbers of people, and especially for the younger third of our adult population, this has in large measure ceased to be true. When I hear people say that "church is boring" or that it's "the last place I'd go for spirituality," when I hear that the church is all about rules and judgment – that really grates on me. I get frustrated, not with those who express such thoughts, but with myself and with the church for not having responded well to the spiritual needs of this generation.

There has been a massive cultural shift over the last 50 years, but many churches that I have experienced are set up to respond to the needs of those who came of age in the 1950s, '60s and '70s. The scripted worship services, the classical music style, the authority and the committee structures are not bad in and of themselves, but they are of another age, and the demographics of the typical church membership list shows it. The way we do church strikes many in the younger third of our population as "old school" and they have a hard time figuring it out.

There is a growing sense across North America and across denominations that the church needs to change. The model needs to shift in response to a changing environment. That's not impossible – the church has seen many such shifts over the past 2,000 years. But change is hard, especially in an institution that many look to for stability in their lives. It's no coincidence that we use the image of rock for both God and the church. At a recent conference for the clergy of our diocese, our guest speaker spoke of the need for change in the church, but at the same time cautioned us that it takes about 30 years to change the culture of a parish.

It's not the first time I've been faced with the need to shift the model in response to a changing environment. During the 1990s, the technology company I was managing faced a similar issue. We were a telecommunications systems integrator, which meant that we would design, integrate, and install complete telecom networks using products manufactured by others. But during the 1990s, we were starting to get squeezed. The product manufacturers started doing more and more of the system design and integration, and the customers started to do more of their own installation. To survive, we would need a fresh expression of our business model, one that could still take advantage of our core competencies. The solution for us was to shift our business focus to air traffic management and to develop a few key software-based products. This allowed us to continue to exploit our engineering and systems integration capability, but in a market sector where customers were willing to pay for that added value.

It is easier to implement change in a medium-sized company of paid employees than it is in a parish setting, with all of its history and traditions, where the "workers" are volunteers, and with the need to care for people who are affected by any change. Which is why when Bishop John offered me the opportunity to start something new at St. Albans, I was enthusiastic. Some of my colleagues thought I was crazy, but for me this was a once-in-a-lifetime opportunity. Why did I want to take on the church plant at St. Albans?

My motives were many, which is probably a good thing. I always recall the words of one of my seminary professors, who warned us that people with singular motives may well turn out to be fanatics. I certainly had mixed motives. The very first thing that appealed to me was the challenge, for I've always been drawn to challenges, and the building of a new church community would certainly be that. But this was a particular challenge, for it was also an opening to do and to *be* church differently, to experiment, and to explore what it means to be a 21st-century church in an urban North American setting. It would be a learning opportunity, and a chance to build and to be part of a team that would explore new ways of being Christian community together.

Some of my thinking on what it means to be church has been influenced by the emerging church movement. I don't know, perhaps no one knows what this emerging church will look like, but I am convinced, as are many others, that the Spirit of God is doing something new and exciting in the church and within Christianity in our time and place. What is this new thing that is emerging? It is a faith that seeks to be post-denominational, to move beyond the current hodgepodge of Christian denominations, appreciating the value of our different traditions, but moving beyond them to seek unity in diversity. It's a movement away from the problems of hierarchy, power, and control that have plagued our churches in the past, to a more community-based approach that remains rooted in the apostolic tradition. It's a faith that reaffirms its Christ-centredness, but that seeks to better understand who Jesus is, reaching beyond the conventional understandings that we often take for granted. One implication of this Christ-centredness is that the emerging church is a movement of people who seek out those on the margins, who walk with the poor and who get involved with social justice, because that's what Jesus did. But it is also a movement of people who seek to know God, a movement of contemplatives who enter into the mystical dimensions of faith, because Jesus was also a mystic whose words and actions flowed out of an intimate knowledge of God.

For many centuries, our churches have been mostly about belief and about a belonging that is contingent on belief. We constructed belief systems, creeds, doctrines, and articles of faith, and we told people that this is what you must believe. If you believed these things, then you were a member of the church. If you didn't believe these things, then you were outside the church. Now, belief is a good thing, especially when understood in its fuller sense of trusting, of having faith and entering into relationship. But when we take belief in its narrower sense of assent to doctrine or other propositional statements, belief isn't particularly demanding. You can say you believe, and as a result you belong, and that may or may not have much of an impact on your day-to-day life.

But what seems to be emerging is a way of being a follower of Jesus that places less emphasis on doctrinal assent and more emphasis on action and contemplation, which are grounded in relationship and in community. It isn't enough just to be a member, or to believe the right things about God, though these are good. Faith is an encounter with the divine that gives rise to a way of life. It's about engagement in the affairs of this world; it's about action. But that action, the way we live our lives, must be rooted in contemplation, rooted not so much in believing the right things about God, but in experiencing the presence of God in one's own life. Rather than simply believing in God, we seek to know God. And we bring that experience into community, into the lived experience of a community of faith.

To deepen and to grow in living relationship with the one we call God, we do well to draw on the riches of our tradition, on the wisdom of those who have gone before us, in eras that were perhaps more contemplative than our own. That means that the community of St. Albans will continue to draw on the liturgical and sacramental tradition of its Anglican roots, and we will be people soaked in and nourished by both the Bible and Christian orthodoxy. We also draw on other traditions: the contemplative tradition of the Catholic Church and monasticism, the passion and commitment of evangelicals, the openness to the movement of the Spirit found in the Pentecostal tradition, the creativity of worship displayed by mainline Protestants, and music and prayer drawn from the width and the breadth of global Christianity.

Another of my motivations in exploring new ways of being church is to restore the demographic balance. I believe that local churches are at their best when they are multi-generational and when they are an incarnation of the neighbourhood in which they are located. It pains me that in many of our churches there is a missing demographic, the demographic of young adults. One of the first things that I noted about St. Albans was that it was situated in a neighbourhood with a large cohort of 20- and 30-somethings. Here was an opportunity to explore how to be a multi-generational church that could serve as a spiritual home for young adults. That was something I was passionate about, and something that I felt called to do. It's also turned out to be immensely rewarding. Over the past few years, my engagement with young-adult church leaders has taught me much about what it means to be passionate, relevant, inclusive, and hospitable as a church. It also keeps me feeling young, and that's a definite bonus.

When I left home at the age of 17 to go to university, I was graciously received into the loving community of St. James Anglican in Kingston, right on the corner of the Queen's University campus. There, I learned first-hand how the church can be a wonderful complement to and component of university life. It was at once a great community of fellow students and the place where I could interact with people of all ages, something that can be a bit of a rarity on a university campus. It was an environment where I could ask questions, explore doubts, and value the interaction between what I learned on campus and at church. That's why I was excited to discover just how close St. Albans was to the University of Ottawa campus. My hope is that we can provide today's students with the sort of spiritual home and church family that was offered to me a generation ago, a community where they can grow and fully engage their faith as young adults. St. Albans has given me the opportunity to pay forward the gift that I received from the church during my university days.

Yet another reason to take on the position at St. Albans had its roots in the sabbatical year I enjoyed over a decade ago. During that time, in addition to my ill-fated piano lessons, I decided to do some volunteering. I thought it would be a good experience and a way to stretch myself, to spend some time working with those who were homeless. I knew about Centre 454, and so I called the staff to see if I could help out. They agreed to have me volunteer there one morning each week. It was a stretch for me all right – the first time I went in I was scared stiff. After spending most of my adult life as a corporate executive, being at the Centre definitely pulled me out of my comfort zone. It was a good experience, though, one that shaped me for the better and gave me a much-needed awareness of the stories of those dealing with poverty. I never imagined that one day I'd be asked to be the pastor of the church that would also serve as the home of Centre 454. Over the past decade, I've become increasingly passionate about social justice, and especially about the battle to end homelessness in our city. We've got a long way to go, but being part of St. Albans gives me a privileged position on the front lines of that fight.

When I circulated some early manuscripts of this book, one of the questions that often came back was "What is a church plant?" Church plants are still quite rare in my diocese and in the Anglican Church of Canada, and that presents a unique opportunity. I am firmly convinced that the church in North America needs to change to meet the needs of the 21st century, and especially the needs of those who have and will come of age in this era. I am also convinced that our Anglican tradition has a lot to offer. Our liturgical and sacramental roots, the global communion, a broad and inclusive theology, a history of reasoned engagement with the Bible, and a passion for social justice and social service – all of these are great gifts as we seek to follow Jesus and to discover God together.

But how do we change to meet the challenges of our current context? There are many ideas out there, and I've got some of my own, and so do others in our community. We pray and we do our best to discern and follow the lead of the Spirit. But what we also need is a community where we can simply try stuff and see how it works. You might call that a church research and development laboratory. With a new church plant at St. Albans, we have the opportunity, and I believe the vocation, to be a R&D lab for the broader church. By our very nature and novelty, we can try stuff, and if it works, great, if it doesn't, we'll try something else. I think that is a critical task for the church, and one that is difficult for more established or traditional congregations. I love the idea of being an R&D lab for the church. It's quite freeing. Even when we fail, we're providing some useful insights, especially if we're diligent about capturing them and letting them be known. And we *did* have some failures.

From our earliest days as a community, we thought about having a Sunday evening service. Many new churches are opting for Sunday evenings instead of Sunday mornings and it seems to work, at least for the cases that we get to hear about. Though we initially decided to launch our worship on Sunday mornings, the possibility of an eventual second service in the evening was enticing. We knew that Sundays had changed in our society, and we were only too aware of the common lament among church folk about the competition we get from children's sports, Sunday shopping, Sunday work shifts, birthday parties, weekends away, and the like.

So I was primed to start something on Sunday evenings at the earliest opportunity. Our earliest opportunity appeared to be September 2012, our second September, the start of the new year for many people, including the students who would be returning to university in our neighbourhood. Zack and I sat down and sketched out an evening gathering, something a bit less formal and with a bit more music than our morning worship, a service that was intended for a smaller group. We put up a few posters and made some announcements. But we kept things relatively low key, since we didn't really want to draw anyone away from our morning congregation; it wasn't big enough for that yet. We'd start small and let it grow.

The first Sunday of our evening service we had ten people. That seemed encouraging. But the next week, we had fewer. For some who came, single-digit attendance just didn't feel like Sunday worship and so they dropped out. Soon we didn't know whether we were a worship service or a small group. Those preparing sermons and music started to feel a bit discouraged, not sure if the low turnout justified the time and energy spent in advance. By Christmas, our Sunday evening gathering was no more.

It turns out we only did one thing right. Immediately after we took the decision to nix the service, we sat down to figure out what we could learn from the failure. We realized that we had never assembled a core group that was committed to the new idea. We hadn't really figured out *why* we wanted a second service or *who* we were trying to serve. Consequently, we hadn't given the gathering much of an identity or a vision that could be communicated with enthusiasm. We took all this and more to heart, and just over a year later, when the community had grown in size to where it could support a second service, we assembled an evening launch team, put in the time needed to envision, shape, and plan the new venture, and successfully launched our St. Al's @5 Sunday evening service.

It's one thing to have what might be called a program failure, such as our aborted first attempt at gathering on Sunday evenings. You pull the plug, cut your losses, learn from your mistakes, and, if appropriate, you try again. It's much more serious to have a failure in the area of church culture. Cultural missteps can become embedded in the fabric of a community and *may* become much more difficult to turn around.

When we first started the new St. Albans, we had a highly dedicated group of first ten, then 20, then 40 people. Though we were few, we were highly engaged, and when something needed to be done, there was always someone who would step up and do it. We'd pass around a clipboard and within minutes all of the slots for reading, leading prayers, and the other things that happen on Sunday morning were full. We'd call for a Saturday cleaning day to get rid of construction dust and the whole community would show up, brooms and mops in hand. We were excited by the launch of our new community and, as a result, participation and energy levels were high. Without any staff apart from myself, the community was volunteer driven, both in its decision making and when it came to getting things done. It was a great atmosphere and the enthusiasm was contagious, rubbing off on newcomers and visitors who joined our community.

The problem was that we took that highly engaged atmosphere for granted and failed to realize the extent to which it was a consequence of the newness of our venture and of the extraordinary commitment of our initial team. As time passed, members of our core group needed to scale back, understandably, on the time and energy they had been committing to St. Albans. We compensated by hiring staff, a part-time administrator, a cleaner, a musician. Nothing out of the ordinary for a church community, but a subtle shift was taking place. We were moving from being a highly engaged, member-driven community, to a less-engaged community where the staff looked after things. Because engagement had been so strong initially, we had taken it for granted and had failed to be intentional in creating a culture of engagement in our church. At first we didn't even notice. But eventually it became apparent that people just weren't stepping forward to do things the way that they had initially. We had trouble getting readers on Sunday mornings. The kitchen was being left in a mess after coffee hour. The flow of energy and ideas seemed to slow.

There are normal ebbs and flows to community life. But there are also steps that can be taken to facilitate participation and to create a culture of engagement. Once we became aware of the problem, some of our missteps were easy to see. The church leadership section of our website listed only staff. Our system for signing up volunteers for Sunday participation was clunky and difficult to use. Our recruiting efforts for participation started to rely more on guilt than on encouragement and identification of gifts. Our parish council members and other community leaders were unknown to many in our community. We failed to commission new leaders and to thank retiring leaders in ways that were sufficiently visible. We're taking steps now to improve these things as we intentionally seek to reinstate a culture of engagement in our community. It's a work in progress.

We're learning as we go, and that's as it should be in an R&D lab. St. Albans is a community that is constantly evolving, with new people joining us every week. Some are just passing through and some find a home with us for the longer term. It is an awesome community. Lives are changed and relationships are formed. We learn, we laugh, we cry, we grow together. I am constantly humbled by the energy and enthusiasm of our younger folks and by the grace and wisdom of the older people (and sometimes vice versa). I am humbled as well by what God is doing in our midst, as I see people deepening their relationships with the divine and growing in their faith in so many ways. These are good times.

Jesus said, "I came that they may have life and have it abundantly." I believe that the church can and should be a community in which that promised abundance becomes a reality, a catalyst for changing lives and enabling and encouraging people to live to their full potential. That's no easy task. It's a vocation that calls us to be ever attentive to the needs of those both *in* and *around* our church communities, attentive to the ways in which those very human needs are shaped and modulated by the culture of our time and place. That in turn requires us to change with the times, not by abandoning our foundations but by learning innovative ways to express those core beliefs and by finding new ways to include and welcome those who, for a variety of reasons, find a distance between themselves and the community of faith. That's what we try to do in the St. Albans community. Sometimes we do it poorly, but sometimes, by the grace of God, we do it well.

EPILOGUE

Easter

I hadn't seen Nick for a while. His mother was ill and he'd been away looking after her. But it was Easter morning and so he made it to St. Albans. He brought a friend with him whom I'd met once before.

"I've been off methadone for two weeks," the friend told me almost as soon as we met, with a big smile on his face. He was in an addiction recovery program and this was good news. They sat on the couch near the back. The church was packed, so I couldn't see Nick, but I knew that he loved to worship, and this was no ordinary gathering. It was Easter and it was the biggest Sunday morning we'd ever had in the new St. Albans. We were putting chairs into every nook and cranny, and the atmosphere was electric. Midway through the service we celebrated the renewal of baptism with four of our young adults. Then the band launched into some Mumford & Sons.

Clapping breaks out spontaneously from all directions, people singing loudly and moving to the music. The band steps it up a notch: more bass, more drums, more vocal harmonies.

And suddenly Nick comes charging up the aisle to the front, a big smile on his face, and he starts dancing right in front of the communion table, some sort of crazy jig. We reach the chorus of "I Will

Wait." By now everyone is clapping and laughing and singing and smiling as Nick continues with his crazy dance, a modern-day King David, dancing before the Lord with all his might as we sing our offering to God.

Alleluia, Christ is risen. The Lord is risen. Indeed.

Those who do worship planning for a living know that you can't script moments like that. You can't manufacture a spontaneous outbreak of the Holy Spirit. But there are ways that we can *discourage* it from happening. Often our worship can be rigid and formal, tightly scripted. Sometimes it becomes too much of a spectator sport. One of the things that I was hoping to do at St. Albans was to loosen things up a bit, to encourage creativity and spontaneity, participation and exploration. In the Anglican church, we have inherited a wonderful liturgical tradition that is thoughtful, deeply rooted in scripture, and that encourages participation and engagement by means of its call and response format and the regular celebration of the Eucharist. But too often, especially when I ask young people, they tell me that our liturgies are boring. That is not the fault of the liturgy; it just means that we have let things get stale.

There are many ways to put life back into liturgy. I've seen churches that have done it by introducing contemplative elements into worship, and I've seen it done by churches who value a high church tradition. Another approach is to borrow from the evangelical and Pentecostal traditions. At their best, these traditions exude energy, passion, and commitment, which can be fused with a more liturgical approach. Music, which is contemporary both in style and in instrumentation, can play an important role. But it is also important to leave room for spontaneity, to not script the liturgy too tightly, so that there is space for both the Spirit and for Nick to dance in our midst.

Some contemporary churches in the Anglican tradition have been so strongly influenced by the evangelical and Pentecostal traditions that they have largely set aside the traditional liturgy. At St. Albans, our community opted for a different approach. We wanted to borrow from other traditions, but we also wanted worship that was both liturgical and sacramental, as well as being Spirit-filled, contemporary, informal, participatory, creative, experimental, meaningful, passionate, and eclectic. That might sound like a long wish list, but it has come together for us as an authentic expression of our community, and no more so than during Holy Week in 2015.

We follow the lectionary because we value the reading of scripture as part of our worship, and not just the scripture passages that we might pick if it were up to us. But sometimes the lectionary hands us a dilemma and no more so than on Palm Sunday: a long passion gospel, which can take up to 20 minutes to read, a challenge even for those with the longest of attention spans. Many churches adopt a multi-voice, dramatic approach to the reading of this text. We decided to take that one step further. Inspired by the popular lessons and carols format that we use for our Christmas carol service, we opted for a multi-voice dramatic reading of the passion, but broke it into sections with reflections and songs interspersed. That allowed our congregation the time it needed, and provided a variety of avenues and opportunities for each of us to insert ourselves into the drama. You never really know in advance whether something new like that is going to work, but it did, and the power of the moment was there for all to experience when we hit the dramatic centre of the cross, singing "Were You There" with nothing but voices accompanied by hand drums, snapping fingers, and shuffling feet.

Maundy Thursday provided us with the opportunity for a smaller, more intimate gathering around the table as we celebrated the Last Supper and then moved on to the Garden of Gethsemane. Many in our community find our Maundy Thursday service to be the most profound of our Holy Week liturgies. For some, the moment that moves them is when, after sharing the Eucharist, we read the gospel text that takes Jesus and his disciples into Gethsemane. Dimming the lights, we sing together a Leonard Cohen song, imagining it perhaps on the lips of Jesus as he prays, "if it be your will that I speak no more ..."

Moments later, out of the darkness, there is a voice: "My God, my God why have you forsaken me?"

Psalm 22 is read, the altar is stripped, and we are left in silence before the silhouette of a large cross, which has been brought out and placed before us. Some stay a minute; some stay much longer as the liturgy dissolves in silent disarray.

Good Friday worship is a subdued affair. But, even on Good Friday, we went off script. Midway through our meditation on the cross, there was a loud noise at the back of the church. A man banged his way noisily through our doors with his bicycle, shouting, "I want a peanut butter sandwich." Good Friday is a statutory holiday, and that means that many of the support services for those who are homeless are closed, including our own Centre 454 day program in the church basement. Sometimes when the door to Centre 454 is locked, people just come through the church doors instead.

I watch out of the corner of my eye as someone gets up and goes to the back of the church to welcome the sandwich seeker. The sandwich seeker shrugs him off and heads down the stairs to the basement. Not a problem, I'm thinking; the door is locked and he'll be back up in a moment. However, it seems that the door hadn't been locked properly, and now the alarm is going off. Zack, our music director, knows the code, so he gets up and runs to the back of the church to disarm the system. I'm hoping he gets there before security shows up. Meanwhile, I continue with our prayers, slowing my pace, stretching things out long enough so that Zack can get back in time for the next song. It all works out. Zack makes it back, the sandwich seeker uses the washroom and then returns to the street with his bicycle, and we finish our Good Friday service.

Having folks from neighbourhood shelters who belong to our community and who participate in our worship has been a good thing for our congregation. It has shaped us for the better. There is something incredibly eye-opening and life-giving about getting to know people whose circumstances and back-stories are very different from our own. They teach us what it means to be a welcoming community and to practice hospitality. We know that for some people life is hard and lacks stability, and to walk through our doors is an act of courage. They may be with us for a few hours or for a few years. They may disappear and then show up again months later. When they do, we celebrate. One of the reasons we celebrate is that often people who come from a hard place in life have a great deal to teach us about faith. When we say and hear things like "Jesus saves," many of us we think about it in a metaphorical or an anticipatory sense. But for some people in our community, when they say that God saved their life, they mean it literally. They remind us of the power of faith. After our Good Friday service, someone came up to me and said, "You know, at first I was annoyed when that man came in and disrupted the prayers. But then it struck me that our meditation on the cross is really all about how God loves us despite the pain and suffering that we humans are responsible for. If God can do that, then surely we can learn to love someone who causes us a little disruption and inconvenience."

It is also good to have people in our midst who remind us that we are living in an age of authenticity and not authority. Usually on a Sunday morning at St. Albans, we have a time for announcements near the end of the service, before the final hymn. But because we were doing a few extra songs for Easter, and because of the importance of the day, I decided that we wouldn't have any announcements on Easter Sunday. As the person with primary responsibility for liturgy in my tradition, that was well within my authority. But when we reached the point in the service where we normally have announcements, just as I'm about to launch into the final blessing, one of our university students jumps up and steps into the aisle of the church.

"Mark, are we doing announcements today?"

"No, we're not doing announcements today."

"Too bad, I have an announcement to make."

And they proceeded to make an announcement. It was a good but long announcement about an Easter dinner for any who didn't

have an Easter dinner to go to. My immediate reaction was annoy-
ance. But soon, it was almost as if I heard a voice saying, "You may
be annoyed, but this is the church you wanted. Be thankful instead."

After our Easter service, during the coffee hour, I caught up
with four newcomers, all of them journalism students from Carleton
University. As is my habit, I wanted to know how they had come to
be with us that morning. They told me that they had decided to go
to church for Easter, but they didn't know where to go. So they
Googled "Contemporary Church Ottawa" and St. Albans came up
at the top of their search. They looked at a few websites, but they
liked the look of ours and the fact that it was up to date. So they
checked us out on social media, liked the vibe, and decided to join us
for Easter morning. But that was neither the beginning nor the end
of the story. It turns out that they had all been regular churchgoers
in high school, a couple of them members of Anglican churches,
plugged in, involved in music and youth groups. When they arrived
in Ottawa for university, they looked for a church, but couldn't find
one that worked for them. Then they did what so many others do;
they weren't going to go to church out of a sense of duty or obligation, so when nothing seemed to fit, when none of the options felt
like an authentic expression of their spirituality, they stopped looking. It wasn't until near the end of their third year of university that
they connected with us on that Easter morning, enjoyed the vibe,
felt welcome, and joined our community.

Stories like that motivate me. It troubles me to hear about people who drop out of the church because they can't find a community
that allows them an authentic expression of their faith. Sometimes
that applies to Anglicans like these journalism students. But it can
also apply to people from a whole variety of traditions. My experience at St. Albans tells me that denominations are becoming less
important, especially for young adults. In our community, people
who have grown up in the Anglican tradition are in the minority.
We have Catholics, mainline Protestants, evangelicals, Christian
Reform, Pentecostals, almost everything in-between, and a whole

lot else. This is good, for it provides us with a richness and a variety of experiences and practices that we can draw upon and make part of the expression of our worshipping community.

One of the things that we try to provide at St. Albans is a safe place for people who have left other churches to land. Sociologists and pollsters have noted that over the past decade a significant number of young adults have "dropped out of attending church, after going regularly." This phenomenon is taking place across Christian denominations. But as researchers like David Kinnaman of the Barna Group have noted, there are many young evangelicals who are passionate about their faith but who have left the churches they grew up in because they are uncomfortable with the anti-science attitudes, or the hostility towards LGBTQ people. Often these people need a place to land, maybe for a little while as they sort things out, or perhaps for longer. Theologically, the Anglican church, with its history of reasoned engagement with scripture, might be a good fit for some. But people who have grown up in evangelical churches often find a traditional Anglican worship style, with its classical music and formal liturgy, to be, well... just a bit strange. At St. Albans, we have been able to bridge at least some of that gap. We see that reflected in the composition of our community. It's good to be a liturgical church where people feel free to get up and dance once in a while.

Easter 2015 marked the fourth anniversary of our Facebook launch. It's been a good journey, both for me and for our community. Habitually, my attention is focused on what comes next, so it's rare that I take the time to appreciate where we've been. But on that Easter Sunday, in the midst of the most wonderful worship that I've ever experienced, I *did* permit myself a moment of quiet celebration and thanks for the community that we've built up over the past four years.

One of the best things about presiding at worship is that I get a great view of the faces. The face of the man who was living in the hospice of the emergency shelter when he first connected with us, who got up and sang with the band a few times, who joined our parish council but was unable to make any meetings, who disappeared for a while, but who now is back. The atheist student who dropped in for the warm familiarity of a Christmas carol service, discovered faith, and is now considering ordination. The man who turned his life around, decided to be baptized, and then later proposed to his girlfriend right in the middle of one of our services. (She said yes!) The woman whose conversation with that man during our Open Space was the catalyst for his decision to be baptized. My parents, and others like them, who keep asking me when we're going to use the organ more, but who graciously sing along to the band's music even though it's not their style. The gay couple, whose marriage we were finally able to bless at St. Albans, on the tenth anniversary of their civil wedding.

We still have our challenges and our faults, like any other church community. We disappoint and we get things wrong. In our own way, we are responding to the 2,000-year-old call to proclaim the good news in our time and in our place. Planting a new church at St. Albans has been and continues to be a great adventure – a great adventure in learning to live abundantly and encouraging others to do the same. For us, abundant living means living a life that is spiritual, a life that has meaning and is full of purpose. It means living life in relationship with others and in relationship with the divine one, who both permeates and transcends our universe; the one we call God, who against all odds loves us and calls us God's people, and who adopts us as children. No one has seen God; but we believe that God has come to be known most fully in the one named Jesus who walked this earth some 2,000 years ago. We are a small part in a big story, a story that's still unfolding. And who knows where the Spirit will lead us next? But it's been a good four years.

MARK WHITTALL

The Rev. Mark Whittall is the pastor of St. Albans Church and a priest of the Anglican Diocese of Ottawa. He is an engineer by training, and obtained graduate degrees in Theoretical Physics and in Development Economics from Oxford University. His first career was as an engineer and executive in the high-tech sector, rising to the position of CEO and earning recognition as Ottawa's Entrepreneur of the Year in 2000. Soon afterwards he left his business career and turned to the study of theology. He served as Professor, History of Science at Augustine College in Ottawa from 2002 to 2007 and was ordained as an Anglican Priest in 2008. After a brief stay in a rural parish, he was tasked with building a new congregation at St. Albans Church in downtown Ottawa in 2011, where he currently serves as pastor.

A preacher and gifted storyteller, Mark is uniquely qualified to write this book not just by virtue of his personal experience in launching and building this new congregation, but also because of his unique ability to bring insights from the worlds of academia, science, business and theology to bear on the stories which he narrates.

From the St. Alban's website
Mark became the Incumbent of St. Albans on July 1, 2011. Mark was born in Montreal but grew up in Manotick, Ontario. His studies took him to Queen's in Kingston and Oxford in the UK, where he completed degrees in engineering, physics and development economics.

He returned to Ottawa to begin his career in technology and international development in 1987. His work with Intelcan took him to more than forty countries around the world, from the jungles of Africa to the tundra of the Arctic. But in 2005 he returned to school, this time to St. Paul University in Ottawa where he completed his Masters in Pastoral Theology in 2008. Mark was ordained in 2008 and served as Incumbent of the Parish of Huntley in Carp until 2011. Mark is enthusiastic about his return to downtown Ottawa to be the Pastor at St. Albans Church. Now he can bike to work! Ministry at St. Albans provides Mark with and exciting and unique opportunity to engage with a diverse group of people of all ages and backgrounds, including the folks at Centre 454 and students at the University of Ottawa. Mark brings a particular passion for working with children and youth to his ministry, a passion which is evident in his puppet collection!

At home, Mark shares his life with Guylaine, his wife of 20 years, and his two children, Jonathan, 17 and Michelle, 15. In his leisure time he enjoys sports, music and even a bit of quantum physics, and he tries to get away on a canoe camping trip with family and friends every summer.

From Bloomberg.com

Mr. Mark Whittall was the Founder and served as Chairman and Chief Executive Officer of Sybridge Technologies, Inc. Mr. Whittall served as Chief Executive Officer of Intelcan Technosystems Inc. since 1998 and also served as its President, a global provider of Air Traffic Management and Wireless Telecom Solutions, which was recognized as one of Canada's fastest growing high technology companies by the *Financial Post* magazine. He served as Chairman and Director of Intelcan Technosystems Inc. Mr. Whittall is a Professional Engineer. He holds an engineering degree from Queen's University and Masters degrees in both Physics and Economics from Oxford University.

Wood Lake

Imagining, living, and telling the faith story.

WOOD LAKE IS THE FAITH STORY COMPANY.

It has told

• the story of the seasons of the earth, the people of God, and the place and purpose of faith in the world;

• the story of the faith journey, from birth to death;

• the story of Jesus and the churches that carry his message.

Wood Lake has been telling stories for more than 30 years. During that time, it has given form and substance to the words, songs, pictures, and ideas of hundreds of storytellers.

Those stories have taken a multitude of forms – parables, poems, drawings, prayers, epiphanies, songs, books, paintings, hymns, curricula – all driven by a common mission of serving those on the faith journey.